Penny Sumner is an Australian who came to England as a postgraduate student. She did a D.Phil at Oxford and now lives in Newcastle upon Tyne where she teaches creative writing and contemporary literature at the University of Northumbria. Her first publication was a short story in *Reader, I Murdered Him* (The Women's Press, 1989). Another story, 'Dead-Head', which appeared in *Reader, I Murdered Him, Too* (The Women's Press, 1995), was shortlisted for the Crime Writers' Association Short Story Dagger Award. She has written two crime novels, *The End of April* (1993), and *Crosswords* (1995), as well as editing *Brought to Book* (1998), all published by The Women's Press.

Also by Penny Sumner from The Women's Press:

The End of April (1993)
Crosswords (1995)
*Brought to Book: Murderous Stories from the
Literary World* (1998)

The Fruits of Labour

Creativity, Self-Expression
and Motherhood

Penny Sumner, editor

First published by The Women's Press Ltd, 2001
A member of the Namara Group
34 Great Sutton Street, London EC1V OLQ
www.the-womens-press.com

British Library Cataloguing-in-Publication Data
A catalogue record for this book is available from the British Library.

ISBN 0 7043 4629 X

Typeset in Sabon by FiSH, London
Printed and bound in Great Britain by
Cox & Wyman, Reading, Berkshire

Contents

Penny Sumner
Introduction

There 'is no more sombre enemy of good art,' Cyril Connolly pronounced, 'than the pram in the hall'. This was in *Enemies of Promise* (1938), and Connolly's warning was intended not so much for the artist – that creative man working away in his study, or putting the finishing touches to the latest canvas in an attic studio – but his wife, that all-accommodating being, 'intelligent and unselfish enough to understand and respect the working of the unfriendly cycle of the creative imagination'.

Now the woman is an artist herself (as if she hasn't always been), and must consider the effect of the pram on her own creativity. How then does motherhood – the whole issue of motherhood – affect women artists, both those who are mothers and those who are not? And how do these experiences relate to the general experiences of women in society? These were the broad questions that inspired this book.

I am a writer. Pondering the question of whether or not to become a mother as well meant venturing into an exciting, yet daunting, landscape. Was this a place I really wanted to inhabit, I wondered? What would happen to 'me', the person who sits up late into the night, the person who has the time needed in order to turn an idea over and over in her mind? Standing at the edge of this new place, my footing unsure already, it was difficult to assess how much further I wanted to go. A writer, a mother: one might cancel out the other. 'Men,' an insidious voice came whispering across rocky terrain, 'produce; whereas women reproduce.'

I began this project with the knowledge that the question of whether or not to have a child, followed by the decision to try to conceive was reflected in my attitude towards my writing. The subsequent birth of my son and the experience of becoming a mother also had a profound influence on my work, not only in terms of the time and energy that I could devote to it, but also in the scale of my ambitions and choice of subject matter. I found myself asking, were other women's experiences the same? Surely they must be. Not exactly the same, of course, but fairly close?

However, what the pieces in this collection show is just how diverse women's experiences and perceptions of motherhood are. There are no definite answers here, and certainly no rights or wrongs. Reading through these essays and thinking back over many con-versations with women writers, visual artists and performers, what echoes is the refrain: 'Yes, but for *me* motherhood means...' It can mean an added creative impetus; or a dreaded sense of failure, the end of a dream. It can be a decision made easily, even lightly; or it can involve a painful, heartbreaking choice.

Another assumption I had to relinquish was that the experience of women working across the arts would be broadly similar. There would be some differences of course – a writer can (if she has to) set up office on the kitchen table, Jane Austen with a laptop – whereas a painter or a sculptor would require studio space. 'But the visual arts have been much more influenced by bohemia,' one painter explained patiently, stained fingers streaking the air, 'and bohemia is a place primarily invented and inhabited by men.' Not all the artists I contacted felt like this but many did. 'Yes, but,' you will hear them say, 'if motherhood is a taboo area then maybe it's our definition of what constitutes art that needs changing.'

The issue of motherhood can also suggest the need for other sorts of change: political change, social change. 'I personally couldn't bring a child into this world,' one poet told me, 'it's far too dangerous a place.' Becoming a mother – or not becoming one – can prompt a desire to change the way the world works. To speak out, through one's art, against inequalities, injustice, war...

War, that devourer of children, was a spectre raised by many of the women who suggested ideas for this book, and the name most frequently mentioned in this context was that of Käthe Kollwitz (1867–1945). Kollwitz was a brilliant artist who managed to defy the conventions of the time by marrying and having children while continuing with her creative career. But then came the First World War and the death of her beloved son, Peter. The diary entries included in this book chart Kollwitz's almost unbearable sadness and her struggle to create a memorial for her son: 'Made a drawing: the mother letting her dead son slide into her arms. I might make a hundred such drawings and yet I do not get any closer to him. I am seeking him. As if I had to find him in the work.' Motherhood doesn't end; it doesn't come to a conclusion when a child is grown, or when they die.

Production, reproduction: the passing on of life, of experience. These are things all women are familiar with. The baton can be handed on in numerous ways;

by women who are mothers and by those who are not. The voices here are saying many different things, describing a variety of experiences: expressing fears, joys, grievances, achievements. However, what ultimately binds all these voices together is a celebration of women's desire to create, women making their mark on the world. It is a celebration of the fruits of labour.

The Fruits of Labour

Julia Darling
Small Beauties

Today my thirteen-year-old daughter won't go to school because of her spots. My fourteen-year-old desperately needs a new pair of shoes, and has gone to school in a pair of shaky-heeled stilettos. Each morning my writing day starts with a list of worries and demands that every mother is familiar with. But although I will do my best to do the things required of me by my daughters I refuse to let them stop me from writing. Each day I cycle to a room that I rent in the city in which I live. It's a room for writing and thinking in. It's the place where I keep my favourite books and CDs. It's small, but light, overlooks a small park, and it's all mine to leave in whatever state I choose.

When I first started writing I didn't have a room at all. I worked in corners. Then I started borrowing rooms in friends' houses, and later I made myself a cubby-hole under the stairs in a flat. Before I found the room I have now I rented other, less suitable rooms and for a while I even wrote in cafés. It seems to me this search for a 'room of one's own' is an analogy for writing itself. It took me ten years to create the right environment in which to complete a novel. I could not have written it without the mental and physical space in which to explore ideas. The money that I got for my first novel has also provided a modest income. Of course it's not exactly a secure living, but if I do become penniless again I would rather send my daughters to school in secondhand shoes than give up my room.

Paradoxically, it was when my daughters were babies that I made up my mind to 'be a writer'. I had always been passionate about words, and my own mother brought her five children up on a diet of poetry and literature. Our house was full of books, and was also a literary monument, being the house that Jane Austen died in. Although I was not academic, and left school at fifteen, I always found words exciting, a way of escaping into other worlds. Because of the family pencil and paper games we used to play, I associated writing with laughter and delight. In our family my three brothers were sent to private schools and groomed for weighty careers, whereas my sister and I were allowed more imaginative freedom, and were sent to local state schools. In fact, I hardly ever went to school, and played truant whenever I could. I was much more interested in the world outside the school walls and in many ways my lack of knowledge has proved an advantage. It has meant that I have never stopped trying to learn.

At first I wanted to be a visual artist, and went to study fine art in Cornwall, but words were the territory I kept on returning to. I certainly never imagined myself as a mother, and didn't really know how to relate to babies. After I finished my degree I moved to the north of England and messed around, doing a variety of arty jobs, trying to be politically correct, and sometimes writing sad poems about how miserable I was. I fell into motherhood at twenty-seven without really thinking about it. To be honest I don't think I knew what to do with my life, I only knew that I didn't want to carry on doing what I was doing. Becoming a mother was a way of gaining some status and identity. I also needed stability and this seemed to be the best way of getting it. In fact, being pregnant and giving birth to two girls in the space of two and a half years was like losing any identity I ever had.

I went into a kind of mindless, milky state, got very thin, and felt very feeble. I was overwhelmed by the emotional and physical demands of mothering and when I was at home with my young children I felt almost invisible. It was at this time that I started to write; feverishly and emotionally. I wrote poems about my daughters, and about my failing marriage. I wrote diaries and notebooks and letters to myself. I was encouraged by some good female friends who were artists and who let me use a room in their untidy dusty flat while they played with my children. It was a very good arrangement. They enjoyed being with children and playing with them (which was something I found hard to do), and I found the hours spent in their house fortifying and enriching.

In this way I got through the pre-school years, although I did my bit at the mother and toddler groups, the cold parks, the doctors' waiting rooms, and all the other places where women spend their days when they have young children. My writing at this time was furnaced by the great love I felt for my daughters. I had never known a feeling like it. I was obsessed and in love with them, but I found it almost impossible to spend all of my time with them too. A poem I wrote at that time, 'Small Beauties' sums up these feelings of panic and love:

Small Beauties (1988)[1]

Let the milk boil over,
the half filled tins of baked beans sit idle on the table,
children scribble on the walls with crayons,
clothes heap in riotous mountains.

I am reading a book.

Let the bells ring, bills lie unopened,
doors slam open then bash shut, letters unwritten,
plants unwatered, bread get hard as a rock.

I am thinking about the moon.

Let the bank get nasty, the grass grow high,
children decorate themselves with lipstick,
build houses within houses in every room,
pee on the floor, pull dolls' heads off.

I am looking for a door.

Oh come here, you small beauties.
Together we will run across the town moor,
with waving fingers, running for our lives.
You are too small, and too beautiful, to ignore.

I did literally run across the town moor. When my
children reached school age my marriage ended and
I moved out of the marital home into a housing
co-operative for single people. I rented a small, one-
bedroom flat in the basement of a terrace that housed
seven other people. I was the only one with children
living in the co-op and we monopolised the garden in
the summer. I loved my new flat. The rent was very
cheap and the flat felt a long way from the suburban
couply area that I had left. There were lots of adults

to play with my daughters, and they spent half the week in my old house with their father and his new partner, so I suddenly had days of quietness and freedom in which to develop my writing.

Of course, it wasn't always as easy as it sounds. Sometimes I would miss the girls and feel I had lost control of their upbringing. A part of me felt that I wasn't a proper mother, and I felt very different from the other mothers at the school, who seemed never to let their children out of their sight. Around this time I formed the 'Poetry Virgins'; a loose grouping of female performers who performed my work, as well as other women's poetry, at women's events. This immediate outlet for my work was stimulating and exciting, and it also provided me with a social life. A group of us met regularly, usually with copious amounts of wine, and tried out new poems. It was also through the Poetry Virgins that I began to get work as a playwright, at first with youth theatres and amateur groups and later with professional companies.

Although the Poetry Virgins performed sporadically, we were always paid, and this, together with running workshops and receiving play commissions, formed my low income for several years. I was lucky, I think, to escape formal employment, and to always be able to work in a flexible way. The difficulty for me was that I never really stopped working, and my life was chaotic. I wrote in a jumpy, uneven way, scribbling down ideas late at night, or working on commissions at the last moment and feeling very unsatisfied with what I had written. I was constantly making childcare arrangements, driving old and unreliable cars, taking in stray cats that died, getting drunk, trying to be a 'good mother' and often feeling a failure. Yet I never stopped believing that writing was important, and though I knew that I hadn't found my creative voice, I used poetry as a means of communicating my angst as a mother and a woman.

My daughters liked the Poetry Virgins. Our evenings were full of laughter and gossip and they particularly liked poems that were about them. The world of playwriting was very different. I was often writing about subjects outside my experience, and I found the world of theatre tricky and male-dominated. I felt that my identity as a mother was unimportant in that arena, and I struggled to compete with the laddish atmosphere of many of the companies I worked with. The most successful plays I wrote were always for female casts, and with female directors. However, after limping along in this fashion for a few years, I began to feel that I wanted to regain more control over my writing, so I started working on some fiction, without much ambition, but simply for the pleasure of playing with language and pushing myself to listen to the voices inside me.

I applied to Northern Arts to spend a month in Ireland at the Tyrone Guthrie Centre, which is an artists' retreat in Monaghan. I think I submitted some wobbly prose. Anyway, I got an award, and this meant that I would be away from my daughters for a whole month. In many ways it wasn't too difficult to leave them. They already had another home and life with their father. It was harder for me. I was afraid that I might lose them altogether. I knew this was largely paranoia, but it is scary to abandon young children for such a long time.

The first trip to Ireland had a huge effect on me. I was able to face up to the barriers that had stopped me from writing properly. It wasn't easy. I got terribly bored in my beautiful room overlooking a lake. I hated myself and everything I tried to write. I think I believed that as soon as you took away the constraints that stopped you from concentrating, words would flow out of you like a fountain. This was not the case. I struggled through the month, making myself acknowledge the internal censors who looked over my shoulder as I was working, forcing myself to write about things I could hardly face. I came back very homesick, with a short story that I had gouged out of myself with great difficulty. My daughters were fine. They seemed to have hardly noticed my absence, and simply called me 'Dad' for a few days. I felt guilty about my unproductiveness while I had been away. Still, I entered the story (called 'Beyond') into a competition, and was incredulous when it won a thousand pounds. It even won a trophy. I think I realised then what creativity potentially demanded of me. I know I wouldn't have written that story if I hadn't gone to Ireland. It was as if I had discovered another country within myself that I hadn't even begun to explore.

This discovery of my inner landscape was also fuelled by a women-only writing class that I went to, run by the poet Gillian Allnutt and novelist Margaret Wilkinson, aptly called 'Writing From The Inside Out'. It's still going, and I attend whenever I can. The group is not concerned with the outer worlds of money or production, but is simply a gathering of women who explore thoughts and ideas through words, using a whole range of techniques, from automatic writing to drawing.

I started to compile a collection of short stories from work begun at this class, and to submit work regularly to competitions and magazines. However, I also still had to support my daughters and somehow earn an income, so I carried on writing plays, and enabling others to write. My life was messy. I wrote in the cubby-hole under the stairs. It was dark and cramped and people laughed when they saw it. It seemed as if the flat was shrinking as my daughters grew. Also, I had fallen in love with a woman, and the relationship was demanding and intense. It seemed as if there was never enough time. Several people had asked me why I didn't try writing a novel, and I would usually tell them that my brain wasn't big enough. I couldn't imagine finding the space in between dealing with the daily demands of my daughters and my lover. Still, although the stories were picked up by a publisher and were eventually published (*Bloodlines*, Panurge Press), it was evident that there was no money to be made from short fiction. I decided that if I was going to write a novel I would have to carve out the time to do it, and that three months – the time in which I thought I could manage a draft – was too long to leave the girls.

I had a friend in Western Australia who had lived in Newcastle and had encouraged me to write when the girls were babies, so I wrote to him asking if he thought he could fix up somewhere for me to work and for all of us to stay. It was a tall order, now I think about it. But my friend, Bob White, is the Head of English at the University of Western Australia and is hugely enthusiastic about new work and writers. He invited us to stay with him and found me a room to work in. He also fixed up various contacts and readings. And so it was that all four of us set off for Fremantle one cold November day, and found ourselves splashing around in swimming pools in Bali before we arrived at Perth Airport.

It was incredibly hot. My partner spent her days floating in water, trying to keep the girls from burning, or they visited tourist attractions, while I disappeared each day and wrote the first thing that came into my head. It was a lot to ask of her. It may sound glamorous, but being with an eight- and six-year-old every day is hard anywhere. It seemed rather ridiculous for me to go that far and to see hardly anything apart from a tiny room in an old shipping warehouse. I can't remember the girls complaining, but it was hard on my partner. However, once I started I couldn't stop, and by the end of our three months I had about fifty thousand words in no particular chronological order. I was glad that, despite my physical and often mental absence, we had all had an adventure, and that writing could take us all to places we might never otherwise have visited. We returned to Newcastle with brown faces and the girls' swimming skills much improved.

The novel was put neatly on one side of my desk and I continued to try and make money, glancing helplessly at it from time to time. I knew it would never develop in the middle of everything else, so yet again I arranged to go to Ireland, leaving the girls behind. This time it was easier to work there. I had a firm project, and although I didn't feel that I worked hard I did a huge amount. I remember that during that time I spoke to my eldest daughter on the phone, and she asked me how I was doing in my 'hotel'. It made me think of rich women leaving their children with nannies to go on expensive trips. Yet I was not rich at all, and if anything these trips away meant I had to work even harder when I was home.

Then, in 1995, when the novel really felt as if it would never be finished, and I was exhausted from running workshops and trying to keep our lives organised, I was diagnosed with breast cancer. It was a tremendous shock. I was thirty-eight, and my prognosis was not good. The cancer had spread to my lymph nodes.

I had every cancer treatment available on the national health. The diagnosis changed everything. My relationship with my daughters became precious and terribly important, and I was forced to re-evaluate my priorities in the face of my precarious mortality. Also, I moved into a new house with my partner, and the girls' father moved away, so we were all living together fulltime. Yet cancer helped me in many ways. I cast off everything and everyone that was causing me stress, or that I just wasn't enjoying. I decided that all I wanted to do was be a mother and finish my novel. It was surprisingly easy to do this. I wish I could have done it without getting cancer.

After I finished my treatment, I made a third trip to Ireland to work on the novel. I found that being there heightened my awareness and focused my work. I met many creative people and being in a discursive atmosphere sharpened my critical skills. Being ill had made me more interested in living, and in the people around me.

Over the next year I finally finished *Crocodile Soup*, four years after our trip to Australia. In that time I also wrote a play called *Eating the Elephant* about my experience of breast cancer. I am proud of both pieces of work.

As I write this I am about to leave for Ireland again

to work on my second novel. *Crocodile Soup* has just been longlisted for the Orange Prize. The second novel is no easier than the first, and my daughters are teenagers now, even more demanding than ever. In many ways they need me the most now. Each day brings a different crisis to which my partner and I must react. It's a moral minefield. But they are proud of me. That's an interesting development in my life. My daughters are actually quite interested in what I do. Earning money certainly validated my seemingly mad career. Now when I say 'I need to go and write my novel' there is a respectful acceptance that I should be allowed the time and space in which to do it.

As I look back and reflect on how mothering has affected my creativity, I would say that in many ways it has helped me to write. The experience of bringing up children brings you closer to yourself, and is generally incredibly rewarding and interesting. I would like to separate the two roles of 'housewife' and 'mother'. So much parenting gets lost in the endless march of domestic tasks that surrounds the whole business of living. As I get older I have moved away from the role of cleaner and tidier. These days I pay a cleaner, and spend as little time as possible being domestic. For a start, it makes me annoyed, and I tend to nag the girls more when I have a Hoover in my hand. I would rather spend the time I have talking to them, or watching terrible television together, or playing a game, or walking in the park, or lying in the bath. Things do seem much simpler now. I go to my room and write, and then I come home and lie around talking to teenagers.

Since *Crocodile Soup* came out I have been involved in all the usual promotional activities, travelling away from home and doing readings and signings. In the last year I have been away for about three months, leaving my partner in charge of my daughters. Although it's been exciting and interesting, I feel fairly guilty about my absences. I am really needed at home on a daily basis, and the fact that I'm spending so much time away from them, and not writing, makes me uncomfortable. I don't know what the answer to all of this is. I have to keep reminding myself that I have a choice. I can do what I like, and what I like to do is write.

I say this because there are no easy answers, and all creative women with children carry an extra layer of responsibility which creates the need for a constant balancing act. Being creative can sustain you but if you are too busy, things begin to unravel. One tends to think if one hadn't had children then none of this would be a problem, but I cannot imagine who I would be now without my daughters. There would have been no boundary to my obsessiveness and I suspect that I would have lived a much more seedy and excessive kind of existence. I would have lost my emotional tent pegs.

I have written this to myself in an effort to discover what motherhood has really meant to me. It has been hugely important and as creative as writing itself. I have never let my children stop me from doing what I wanted, and so far they seem not to have suffered too badly from my long absences, nor from having many other key relationships with adults who are not their parents.

I have a poetry book on my shelf called *Moving into the Space Cleared by Our Mothers*, by the Irish writer Mary Dorcey. I am fond of this title and like to repeat it to myself. I hope that my daughters will inherit the mental space I have created and that the flaws in my mothering skills will be overlooked in the long term, when they come into this inheritance. I think the feelings that I have always had around my children have deepened my emotional geography. Oddly, I don't think I would have been a writer without them.

1   The poem 'Small Beauties' was first published in *Modern Goddess*, Julia Darling and Ellen Phethean (eds), Diamond Twig Press, 1993.

Maggie Gee
To My Daughter

To be read after your 21st birthday, 2007

Dearest Rosa

Now you are grown up I am writing you a letter that
I hope won't come out as a succession of apologies,
which strikes an apologetic note straight away. A
working mother's place is in the wrong; we all know
that. But I bet I apologise at least once more before
this letter is through.

I am writing to tell you what it felt like to be a
mother and a novelist. Though I would be more
interested to know what it was like from your point
of view, truthfully. (Hang on; how much truth could I
take?)

I want to say first that for a woman it is still the
greatest luck to be able to work at something you love
and also have a family. My mother, your green-eyed
gypsyish Grandma Aileen, did not enjoy the same
luck, though for a while she taught in your
grandfather's school. She was clever and organised,
and could have done anything, but with three
children, and married to a man who needed to be the
breadwinner and liked to have a wife at home, she
had few choices. Her mother, your great-grandmother,
certainly both worked and had a family, because she
came from the working class, but raising seven

children while working as a domestic servant was not an easy life.

Whereas being a novelist is surely light work. Or is it?

You know it isn't, darling, because you have seen the piles of drafts spread over the floor; you've heard, probably with increasing scepticism, the number of times your mother has announced 'I've finished!' – only to set off polishing and cutting again. You remember how the sheer number of hours at my computer gave me crippling repetitive strain injury, so that for a few months I couldn't pick you up or cuddle you or shop. You remember both the good days when I was earning a lot of money from my novels, and the less good days when I was frustrated by having to do endless reviewing, lecturing and examining to pay my half of our enormous mortgage while also trying to live my real life as a writer and a mother.

I always told you that having a daughter was the best thing in the world. But how could you square that with what you must have sometimes noticed was my impatience to get on with my work, my eagerness for you to go and play or stay with friends, my unwillingness to prolong bedtime chats because I knew I still had work to do before my own bedtime, my complaints that you and your father left the dirty work in the house to me. I complained, God, how I complained. I have always detested housework, but I like a pretty, welcoming, orderly house; it matters to me much more than it does to you and your father, so maybe it was fair enough that I had to make it happen. But I hope you will either live in a tent or be rich enough to pay other people (well) to do that donkey-work for you, so that you can spend your time on more enjoyable things, like love and your real work.

It would be silly to deny that powerful mothers can be a problem (though even as I write, I can imagine your face grinning at me and saying, 'So you think you're powerful, Mum? Big mistake...!') But the problem was very clear to me when you said wistfully, still at primary school, a day or two after some conversation among the adults about my absurdly over-academic past, 'Mummy, do I have to get four degrees?' I was horrified, and saddened (and said 'No, no, no – for heaven's sake, I only did what I did to please my mother, whose family had no money to send her to college, and we can't carry on like that for ever, passing duties across the generations'). But your question made me understand something that stood me in good stead afterwards; you had to know that your path was your path, and not mine.

I confided in you about the balancing act between love and work long before you should have had to think about things like that. And I know how much I admired your amazing good sense and independence of mind when you said, as I wheeled you along in your pushchair one day and wittered and worried to you about my work, 'Big people can't be friends with little people.' You had to say it twice before I took it in. You were telling me what I should have known, but had temporarily forgotten. And you were only three. But of course, when you were not yet two, and just starting to use sentences, I helped you out of the bath one day and you stood there gleaming and dripping wet and said to me with an enormous gummy grin of astounded realisation, 'I'm a person! I'm a person!' You always were.

I went through a long bad patch with my work when you were between nine and twelve. It coincided with a time of climactic change at your father's workplace, and you knew we were worried about money. Should we have hidden it from you? Probably. It was a lot for you to take, but my feeling was that it would be worse for you to see me depressed and anxious and not know why. I only knew you felt all right about it again when my new novel had come out and been well reviewed, and you started feeling safe enough to make rude jokes once more about your mother's general incompetence.

When were the worst days?

When I had a deadline and you were ill and couldn't go to school, so I neither looked after you, nor did my work, as well as I should have done. Luckily after your first few years you became robustly healthy and rarely had days off. Which makes me consider my own mother's saintly patience, looking after a daughter who was almost never at infant school in winter because of asthma, and who malingered considerably throughout her teens. I particularly remember my 'tickle your nose with a hair-grip' technique for making myself sneeze. Mum always pretended to be fooled. Perhaps she liked my company. I love your company too, but I saw schooldays as a heaven-sent opportunity to work without neglecting you – so I was not the most amenable of mothers to hints about bunking off.

There were days when the balancing act didn't work. The year at primary school when suddenly you, always sociable and gregarious, didn't have anyone to play with, and would say, every night it seemed, just as I was tiptoeing away from your bedside, in a small determined voice, 'I didn't have anyone to play with at playtime today.' It always cramped my stomach with anxiety and brought me back, to reassure you, in theory, but actually to reassure myself. Because when I was your age, friendlessness was a permanent and horrible state. Although I always told you it wouldn't last, in my heart of hearts I was afraid you were going to be like me. And then with that fear in my breast I couldn't work later. (I know this sounds as though I'm saying it hurt me more than it hurt you, which is rubbish; but I think parents are always worse at coping with their children suffering in the same way as they did. In any case, in the end you weren't really at all like me, were you? That period passed away like a dream. You make friends easily now, and keep them.)

Other bad moments. When I was asked to go on a six-week reading tour of Tasmania and Australia, and my publisher, herself a mother, offered to send you with me. In theory it was a wonderful offer, but in practice it would have been a nightmare, because I could never manage to be a performing writer and a mother at the same time; I should have been torn in two. I said no to her offer, and yes to the reading tour, but dropped out two weeks before the event, with deep shame, because I couldn't bear to leave you for so long; you were only four or five I think.

What else? When I was trying to talk to publishers or commissioning editors on the phone when you were small, and you, regular as clockwork, came and tried to reclaim me, snatching the phone, talking loudly or wailing with jealousy, to the consternation of the person on the other end of the line.

When I felt completely split about whether or not to accept an invitation to travel, because I have never liked leaving you. It shows, in retrospect, in the letters and postcards I wrote to you every day when I did go away for a week to teach or write. Some of them survive, and when I look at them now, I see they are full of love, but also reek of guilt – trying too hard, in the way that Sylvia Plath's letters home to her mother have false notes of guilt and trying to be good. Guilt can go both ways between the generations, it seems. I hope you only noticed the love.

And yet I cannot deny that I adore having time completely alone, because then I can imagine things in a different way, with infinitely greater clarity and boldness. The mother and the writer seem to live in two very different parts of my brain. I am amazed by Fay Weldon saying she wrote best at the kitchen table while breast-feeding a baby, because I write best in my study with the door closed. Until you were about ten I never tried to do my real writing while you were in the house, unless you were asleep, that is. The mother has to be pliable, adaptable, other-centred, personal, emotional; the writer needs detachment and a degree of steel.

What were the best times?

I know perfectly well that sometimes you were proud of me and glad that your mother did something interesting.

When you came home from school and were happy to see me there, and I'd had my working day and was happy to see you too. 'Any goss, Rosa?' I would say (goss was our word for gossip), and we would exchange whatever we had over tea and crumpets. The unparalleled happiness then of knowing I had both work and love.

When something at work had gone well and we celebrated as a family, perhaps with an evening walk and picnic in the sunset park and a game of Roundwood Rounders in the big circle of plane trees.

When you came to a reading I did once, because our babysitting plans had broken down, and I read a short extract from the new book, as per usual, and then, at the end of the session, asked the audience if there were any more questions, and you put your hand up and said urgently, 'Will you read the rest of the story?'

When you made me glorious multicoloured, starred and stickered, capitalised and exclamation-mark-dotted cards to say 'Well done' at the end of a book. (I have them all, darling. Shall keep them always.)

When, without my knowing you were doing it, you read the first chapter of a book I had had problems with and said to me, 'I really want to read this book. I think it's going to be my favourite.'

When you showed your rare qualities of empathy and imagination and somehow treated me as a person as well as your mother. 'I'm a person,' remember? Perhaps because you felt that way about yourself, you could sometimes give me the same licence. Sometimes, of course, you couldn't, and rightly so, because you just needed a mother, and not to have to think about the rest. Children have a right to more needs than mothers.

Did things get easier as you got older? Not necessarily. Babies sleep a lot; teenagers hardly seem to sleep at all. Teenagers have house-sized personalities and need heart-to-hearts at midnight. Teenagers love and hate volcanically and can strip the parental ego to nothing in seconds . . . On the other hand, something else is beginning. Both of you can see the end is in sight.

You became more precious as you became more difficult. You, my beloved child, were going beyond me, finding your own goals, your own peers, your own satisfactions. You started to get creative pleasure from your own projects: directing a play, writing a long short story, cooking an elaborate meal, making a denim shoulderbag dripping with stars and sequins, safety-pins and peace badges.

Have I made it sound, in this letter, as though there is always a tussle between motherhood and creativity? If so, I have sold motherhood short. There is a tussle for time, true. Two lives would be better than one. But if I had not had a child, half of the one life we get would have been closed to me. There is a freemasonry of parents, chatting in the park by the sandpit in the green slow summer, complaining round the school gate at sunset in winter, laughing in the kitchen over a cup of tea about the things we are failing to get right, which I could never have joined without you. There are kinds of tenderness I should not have known. I would never have understood my place in a chain of lives, a pattern of history, if I had not carried that line on into the future. You helped me to understand what small amount I have managed to understand about this life. Your presence is in my novels *Grace* and *Lost Children*, and your absence – by which I mean what you have taught me about childlessness – is at the centre of *Where Are the Snows* and *The Ice People*.

I don't know if having a creative mother makes it easier or harder to be creative yourself. I know I haven't encouraged you to write novels, although you write with wonderful ease and fluency and in a quite different style from me, because I don't think children should be what their parents have been, and because I'm not sure if someone sociable should ever be a novelist. But if that's what you want to be I hope you'll do it and completely ignore your mother's discouragement.

I know that because my life has been shadowed by money worries I have probably emphasised too much with you the importance of financial security, a subject which my parents never once broached with me. The trouble is, parents want their children to be rich, happy and creative; but also idealistic, thoughtful and sensible. We want everything for you, but fortunately have neither the right to ask it, nor the power to give it, because in the end you have to do everything for yourself, find your own way, and fall into your own errors just as I still fall into mine.

Finally, I want to repeat that you have been the best thing I have made (with your father's help) and also the most original and unpredictable, because, thank goodness, unlike my novels, you are not under my control. You are yourself. I hope you know that still, and can be yourself with more ease and less of a struggle than your mother could. I wish you both motherhood and creativity, in whatever field. I hope you carry on the slim but strong female line in our largely male family, I hope you catch on earlier than I did how fantastic having children is, and so manage to have more than I did, because I have wished very much that you had a sister or brother to fight and have fun with. I wish you a man both as loving as your father is, and as committed to letting the mother of the family have a life, and space, of her own. I hope you feel the beauty and strangeness of life as strongly as I do, but in your own way.

And here comes that apology: I am sorry for all the things I got wrong; they were because I knew no

better or could do no better. I bet that you yourself
will do better, and I hope I live long enough to see it.
I shall always love you with all my heart.

Your mother

Louise Erdrich
from **The Blue Jay's Dance**

Once again my roses are blooming outside the window, a tough rugosa called Therese Bugnet. Their full, glowing, pink heads droop directly outside the screen, heavy with last night's rain – their fragrance a clear, unspeakable luscious berry, sweet as thunder. The churr of wood frogs is still loud in the night. Clouds darken in the north. Storms hammer down from Quebec. The sky crackles, a Cellophane sheath crumpled suddenly overhead. Gnats, bloodsucking, hairline loving, bite raw welts into our napes. On the outermost petal of the farthest blossom, I spy something black, large, and velvet. A huge spider made of plush. It is an opulent thing, its legs thick and curved, its eyes blue glowing spots. There's a screen between the two of us. Still, I am startled when it jumps. It moves with such mechanical and purposeful energy. Blossom to blossom, stuffing aphids into its jaws with thick limbs, mandibles clashing, it hunts.

When mating, these blue-eyed jumping spiders hold hands in the classic stance of either bashful lovers or wrestlers lethally balanced. If the male is not deeply vigilant and ready to leap backward as soon as he has succeeded in delicately thrusting the packet of his sperm into – what shall I call it – his lady's love chamber, she will grasp him closer, killingly, loving him to death, making a meal of him with her sudden sexually quickened appetite. To her, devouring her mate is a bit like smoking a cigarette after sex. That is why the male so tenderly clings to her hands, her tough pincers – he is trying both to make love to her and to survive her.

The example of the spider's courtship, like that of the praying mantis who cannibalises her mate, fascinates because it seems so improbable in its contrast to our human arrangements in which men are physically the stronger and in most cases still dominate the world despite our hopeful advances, our power feminism.

Women writers live rose nights and summer storms, but like the blue-eyed jumping spider opposite our gender, must often hold their mates and families at arm's length or be devoured. We are wolf spiders, carrying our babies on our backs, and we move slowly but with more accuracy. We learn how to conserve our energy, buy time, bargain for the hours we need.

Every female writer starts out with a list of other female writers in her head. Mine includes, quite pointedly, a mother list. I collect these women in my heart and often shuffle through the little I know of their experiences to find the toughness of spirit to deal with mine.

Jane Austen – no children, no marriage. Mary Wollstonecraft – died in childbirth. Charlotte Brontë – died of hyperemesis gravidarum, a debilitating and uncontrollable morning sickness. Anne Brontë and Emily Brontë – no children or marriage. George Eliot, a.k.a. Mary Ann Evans – banned from society for an illicit liaison with a married man. No children. George Sand, Harriet Beecher Stowe, Elizabeth Gaskell – children. Emily Dickinson – no children, no marriage.

Virginia Woolf – no children. Willa Cather, Jean Rhys, Djuna Barnes, Isak Dinesen – none. Kay Boyle and Meridel LeSueur – many children and political lives. Sigrid Undset, children, and Anna Akhmatova. Zora Neale Hurston, Dorothy Parker, Lillian Hellman. None. None. None. Grace Paley, Tillie Olsen – children. Toni Morrison – children. Anne Sexton. Adrienne Rich – children. Anne Tyler, Erica Jong, Alice Walker, Alice Munro, and Alice Hoffman. Children. Joan Didion. Mary Gordon. Rosellen Brown, Robb Forman Dew, and Josephine Humphreys and Mona Simpson. Children. Isabel Allende, Jayne Anne Phillips, Linda Hogan, Sharon Olds, Louise Glück, Jane Smiley, and many, many others.

Reliable birth control is one of the best things that's happened to contemporary literature – that can be seen from the list above. Surely, slowly, women have worked for rights and worked for respect and worked for emotional self-sufficiency and worked for their own work. Still it is only now that mothers in any number have written literature. I beg a friend to send me Jane Smiley's thoughts on the subject – 'Can Mothers Think?' In this piece, she speculates on writing and motherhood, upon what we do write, what we will write, how it will be different.

A mother's vision would encompass survival, she says, *would encompass the cleaning up of messes*.

A mother's vision includes tough nurturance, survival love, a demanding state of grace. It is a vision slowly forming from the body of work created by women. I imagine a wide and encompassing room filled with women lost in concentration. They are absorbed in the creation of an emotional tapestry, an intellectual quilt. Here a powerful blossom forms, there a rushing city, a river so real it flows, a slow root, a leaf. And, too, pieces that do not seem to fit into the scheme at all incorporate themselves in startling ways.

There is labour itself – birth as original a masterpiece as death. There is the delicate overlapping flower of another human personality forming before your eyes, and you blessed and frightened to be part of it. There is the strange double vision, the you and not you of a genetic half replicated in the physical body of another – your eyebrows appear, your mother's heart line, your father's crooked little finger. There is the tedious responsibility of domesticity that alternates with a hysterical sense of destined fate – the bigness and the smallness.

Writing as a mother shortly after bearing, while nurturing, an infant, one's heart is easily pierced. To look full face at evil seems impossible, and it is difficult at first to write convincingly of the mean, the murderous, the cruelty that shadows mercy and pleasure and ardour. But as one matures into a fuller grasp of the meaning of parenthood, to understand the worst becomes a crucial means of protecting the innocent. A mother's tendency to rescue fuels a writer's careful anger.

The close re-experiencing of childhood's passions and miseries, the identification with powerlessness, the apprehension of the uses of power, flow inevitably from a close relationship with a son or daughter. Perhaps most shaking, the instinct to protect becomes overwhelming. A writer's sympathies, like forced blooms, enlarge in the hothouse of an infant's need. The ability to look at social reality with an unflinching mother's eye, while at the same time guarding a helpless life, gives the best of women's work a savage coherence.

Rather than submit her child to slavery, Toni Morrison's Sethe kills her daughter, an act of ruthless mercy. The contradiction, purity, gravity of mother love pulls us all to earth.

'Too thick,' says a character of Sethe's mother love, 'too thick'.

Sigrid Undset's extraordinary Kristin Lavransdatter, a woman whose life is shaped by powerful acts of love, commits sins unthinkable for her time and yet manages to protect her children.

'Milk brain,' a friend calls these maternal deep affections that prime the intellect. Milk wisdom. Milk visions.

I exist, I simply breathe, I do nothing but live.

One day as I am holding baby and feeding her, I realise that this is exactly the state of mind and heart that so many male writers from Thomas Mann to James Joyce describe with yearning – the mystery of an epiphany, the sense of oceanic oneness, the great *yes*, the wholeness. There is also the sense of a self merged and at least temporarily erased – it is deathlike. I close my eyes and see Frost's too peaceful snowy woods, but realise that this is also the most alive place I know – Blake's gratified desire. These are the dark places in the big two-hearted river, where Hemingway's Nick Adams won't cast his line, the easeful death of the self of Keats's nightingale. Perhaps we owe some of our most moving literature to men who didn't understand that they wanted to be women nursing babies.

Adrienne Rich
Anger and Tenderness
from Of Woman Born

In a living room in 1975, I spent an evening with a group of women poets, some of whom had children. One had brought hers along, and they slept or played in adjoining rooms. We talked of poetry, and also of infanticide, of the case of a local woman, the mother of eight, who had been in severe depression since the birth of her third child, and who had recently murdered and decapitated her two youngest, on her suburban front lawn. Several women in the group, feeling a direct connection with her desperation, had signed a letter to the local newspaper protesting the way her act was perceived by the press and handled by the community mental health system. Every woman in that room who had children, every poet, could identify with her. We spoke of the wells of anger that her story cleft open in us. We spoke of our own moments of murderous anger at our children, because there was no one and nothing else on which to discharge anger. We spoke in the sometimes tentative, sometimes rising, sometimes bitterly witty, unrhetorical tones and language of women who had met together over our common work, poetry, and who found another common ground in an unacceptable, but undeniable anger. The words are being spoken now, are being written down; the taboos are being broken, the masks of motherhood are cracking through.

For centuries no one talked of these feelings. I became a mother in the family-centered, consumer-oriented, Freudian-American world of the 1950s. My husband spoke eagerly of the children we would have; my parents-in-law awaited the birth of their grandchild. I had no idea of what *I* wanted, what *I* could or could not choose. I only knew that to have a child was to assume adult womanhood to the full, to prove myself, to be 'like other women'.

To be 'like other women' had been a problem for me. From the age of thirteen or fourteen, I had felt I was only acting the part of a feminine creature. At the age of sixteen my fingers were almost constantly ink-stained. The lipstick and high heels of the era were difficult-to-manage disguises. In 1945 I was writing poetry seriously and had a fantasy of going to postwar Europe as a journalist, sleeping among the ruins in bombed cities, recording the rebirth of civilisation after the fall of the Nazis. But also, like every other girl I knew, I spent hours trying to apply lipstick more adroitly, straightening the wandering seams of stockings, talking about 'boys'. There were two different compartments, already, to my life. But writing poetry, and my fantasies of travel and self-sufficiency, seemed more real to me; I felt that as an incipient 'real woman' I was a fake. Particularly was I paralysed when I encountered young children. I think I felt men could be – wished to be – conned into thinking I was truly 'feminine'; a child, I suspected, could see through me like a shot. This sense of acting a part created a curious sense of guilt, even though it was a part demanded for survival.

I have a very clear, keen memory of myself the day after I was married: I was sweeping a floor. Probably the floor did not really need to be swept; probably I simply did not know what else to do with myself. But as I swept that floor I thought: 'Now I am a woman. This is an age-old action, this is what women have always done.' I felt I was bending to some ancient form, too ancient to question. *This is what women have always done.*

As soon as I was visibly and clearly pregnant, I felt, for the first time in my adolescent and adult life, not-guilty. The atmosphere of approval in which I was bathed – even by strangers on the street, it seemed – was like an aura I carried with me, in which doubts, fears, misgivings, met with absolute denial. *This is what women have always done.*

Two days before my first son was born, I broke out in a rash which was tentatively diagnosed as measles, and was admitted to a hospital for contagious diseases to await the onset of labour. I felt for the first time a great deal of conscious fear, and guilt toward my unborn child, for having 'failed' him with my body in this way. In rooms near mine were patients with polio; no one was allowed to enter my room except in a hospital gown and mask. If during pregnancy I had felt in any vague command of my situation, I felt now totally dependent on my obstetrician, a huge, vigorous, paternal man, abounding with optimism and assurance, and given to pinching my cheek. I had gone through a healthy pregnancy, but as if tranquillised or sleep-walking. I had taken a sewing class in which I produced an unsightly and ill-cut maternity jacket which I never wore; I had made curtains for the baby's room, collected baby clothes, blotted out as much as possible the woman I had been a few months earlier. My second book of poems was in press, but I had stopped writing poetry, and read little except household magazines and books on childcare. I felt myself perceived by the world simply as a pregnant woman, and it seemed easier, less disturbing, to perceive myself so. After my child was born the 'measles' were diagnosed as an allergic reaction to pregnancy.

Within two years, I was pregnant again, and writing in a notebook:

November 1956
Whether it's the extreme lassitude of early pregnancy or something more fundamental, I don't know; but of late I've felt, toward poetry – both reading and writing it – nothing but boredom and indifference. Especially toward my own and that of my immediate contemporaries. When I receive a letter soliciting mss., or someone alludes to my 'career', I have a strong sense of wanting to deny all responsibility for and interest in that person who writes – or who wrote.

If there is going to be a real break in my writing life, this is as good a time for it as any. I have been dissatisfied with myself, my work, for a long time.

My husband was a sensitive, affectionate man who wanted children and who – unusual in the professional, academic world of the 1950s – was willing to 'help'. But it was clearly understood that this 'help' was an act of generosity; that *his* work, *his* professional life, was the real work in the family; in fact, this was for years not even an issue between us. I understood that my struggles as a writer were a kind of luxury, a peculiarity of mine; my work brought in almost no money: it even cost money, when I hired a household helper to allow me a few hours a week to write. 'Whatever I ask he tries to give me,' I wrote in March 1958, 'but always the initiative has to be mine.' I experienced my depressions, bursts of anger, sense of entrapment, as burdens my husband was forced to bear because he loved me; I felt grateful to be loved in spite of bringing him those burdens.

But I was struggling to bring my life into focus. I had never really given up on poetry, nor on gaining some control over my existence. The life of a Cambridge tenement backyard swarming with children, the repetitious cycles of laundry, the nightwakings, the interrupted moments of peace or of engagement with ideas, the ludicrous dinner parties at which young wives, some with advanced degrees, all seriously and intelligently dedicated to their children's welfare and their husbands' careers, attempted to reproduce the amenities of Brahmin Boston, amid French recipes and the pretence of effortlessness – above all, the ultimate lack of seriousness with which women were regarded in that world – all of this defied analysis at that time, but I *knew* I had to remake my own life. I did not then understand that we – the women of that academic community – as in so many middle-class communities of the period – were expected to fill both the part of the Victorian Lady of Leisure, the Angel in the House, and also of the Victorian cook, scullery maid, laundress, governess, and nurse. I only sensed that there were false distractions sucking at me, and I wanted desperately to strip my life down to what was essential.

June 1958
These months I've been all a tangle of irritations deepening to anger: bitterness, disillusion with

society and with myself; beating out at the world, rejecting out of hand. What, if anything, has been positive? Perhaps the attempt to remake my life, to save it from mere drift and the passage of time...

The work that is before me is serious and difficult and not at all clear even as to plan. Discipline of mind and spirit, uniqueness of expression, ordering of daily existence, the most effective functioning of the human self – these are the chief things I wish to achieve. So far the only beginning I've been able to make is to waste less time. That is what some of the rejection has been all about.

By July of 1958 I was again pregnant. The new life of my third – and, as I determined, my last – child, was a kind of turning for me. I had learned that my body was not under my control; I had not intended to bear a third child. I knew now better than I had ever known what another pregnancy, another new infant, meant for my body and spirit. Yet, I did not think of having an abortion. In a sense, my third son was more actively chosen than either of his brothers; by the time I knew I was pregnant with him, I was not sleepwalking any more.

August 1958 (Vermont)
I write this as the early rays of the sun light up our hillside and eastern windows. Rose with [the baby] at 5:30 am and have fed him and breakfasted. This is one of the few mornings on which I haven't felt terrible mental depression and physical exhaustion.

...I have to acknowledge to myself that I would not have chosen to have more children, that I was beginning to look to a time, not too far off, when I should again be free, no longer so physically tired, pursuing a more or less intellectual and creative life ... The *only* way I can develop now is through much harder, more continuous, connected work than my present life makes possible. Another child means postponing this for some years longer – and years at my age are significant, not to be tossed lightly away.

And yet, somehow, something, call it Nature or that affirming fatalism of the human creature, makes me aware of the inevitable as already part of me, not to be contended against so much as brought to bear as an additional weapon against drift, stagnation and spiritual death. (For it is really death that I have been fearing – the crumbling to death of that scarcely-born physiognomy which my whole life has been a battle to give birth to – a recognisable, autonomous self, a creation in poetry and in life.)

If more effort has to be made then I will make it. If more despair has to be lived through, I think I can anticipate it correctly and live through it.

Meanwhile, in a curious and unanticipated way, we really do welcome the birth of our child.

There was, of course, an economic as well as a spiritual margin which allowed me to think of a third child's birth not as my own death-warrant but as an 'additional weapon against death'. My body, despite recurrent flares of arthritis, was a healthy one; I had good prenatal care; we were not living on the edge of malnutrition; I knew that all my children would be fed, clothed, breathe fresh air; in fact it did not occur to me that it could be otherwise. But, in another sense, beyond that physical margin, I knew I was fighting for my life through, against, and with the lives of my children, though very little else was clear to me. I had been trying to give birth to myself; and in some grim, dim way I was determined to use even pregnancy and parturition in that process.

Before my third child was born I decided to have no more children, to be sterilised. (Nothing is removed from a woman's body during this operation; ovulation and menstruation continue. Yet the language suggests a cutting- or burning-away of her essential womanhood, just as the old word 'barren' suggests a woman eternally empty and lacking.) My husband, although he supported my decision, asked whether I was sure it would not leave me feeling 'less feminine'. In order to have the operation at all, I had to present a letter, counter-signed by my husband, assuring the committee of physicians who approved such operations that I had already produced three children, and stating my reasons for having no more. Since I had had rheumatoid arthritis for some years, I could give a reason acceptable to the male panel who sat on my case; my own judgement would not have been acceptable. When I awoke from the operation, twenty-four hours after my child's birth, a young nurse looked at my chart and remarked coldly: 'Had yourself spayed, did you?'

The first great birth-control crusader, Margaret Sanger, remarks that of the hundreds of women who wrote to her pleading for contraceptive information in the early part of the twentieth century, all spoke of wanting the health and strength to be better mothers to the children they already had; or of wanting to be physically affectionate to their husbands without dread of conceiving. None was refusing motherhood altogether, or asking for an easy life. These women – mostly poor, many still in their teens, all with several children – simply felt they could no longer do 'right' by their families, whom they expected to go on serving and rearing. Yet there always has been, and there remains, intense fear of the suggestion that women shall have the final say as to how our bodies are to be used. It is as if the suffering of the mother, the primary identification of woman *as* the mother – were so necessary to the emotional grounding of human society that the mitigation, or removal, of that suffering, that identification, must be fought at every level, including the level of refusing to question it at all.

'Vous travaillez pour l'armee, madame?' (You are working for the army?), a Frenchwoman said to me early in the Vietnam war, on hearing I had three sons.

April 1965
Anger, weariness, demoralisation. Sudden bouts of weeping. A sense of insufficiency to the moment and to eternity...

Palalysed by the sense that there exists a mesh of relations, between, eg, my rejection and anger at [my eldest child], my sensual life, pacifism, sex (I mean in its broadest significance, not merely physical desire) – an interconnectedness which, if I could see it, make it valid, would give me back myself, make it possible to function lucidly and passionately – Yet I grope in and out among these dark webs –

I weep, and weep, and the sense of powerlessness spreads like a cancer through my being.

August 1965, 3.30 am
Necessity for a more unyielding discipline of my
   life.
Recognise the uselessness of blind anger.
Limit society.
Use children's school hours better, for work &
   solitude.
Refuse to be distracted from own style of life.
Less waste.
Be harder & harder on poems.

Once in a while someone used to ask me, 'Don't you
ever write poems about your children?' The male
poets of my generation did write poems about their
children – especially their daughters. For me, poetry
was where I lived as no one's mother, where I existed
as myself.

The bad and the good moments are inseparable for
me. I recall the times when, suckling each of my
children, I saw his eyes open full to mine, and realised
each of us was fastened to the other, not only by
mouth and breast, but through our mutual gaze: the
depth, calm, passion, of that dark blue, maturely
focused look. I recall the physical pleasure of having
my full breast suckled at a time when I had no other
physical pleasure in the world except the guilt-ridden
pleasure of addictive eating. I remember early the
sense of conflict, of a battleground none of us had
chosen, of being an observer who, like it or not, was
also an actor in an endless contest of wills. This was
what it meant to me to have three children under the
age of seven. But I recall too each child's individual
body, his slenderness, wiriness, softness, grace, the
beauty of little boys who have not been taught that

the male body must be rigid. I remember moments of peace when for some reason it was possible to go to the bathroom alone. I remember being uprooted from already meagre sleep to answer a childish nightmare, pull up a blanket, warm a consoling bottle, lead a half-asleep child to the toilet. I remember going back to bed starkly awake, brittle with anger; knowing that my broken sleep would make next day a hell, that there would be more nightmares, more need for consolation, because out of my weariness I would rage at those children for no reason they could understand. I remember thinking I would never dream again (the unconscious of the young mother – where does it entrust its messages, when dream-sleep is denied her for years?)

For many years I shrank from looking back on the first decade of my children's lives. In snapshots of the period I see a smiling young woman, in maternity clothes or bent over a half-naked baby; gradually she stops smiling, wears a distant, half melancholy look, as if she were listening for something. In time my sons grew older, I began changing my own life, we began to talk to each other as equals. Together we lived through my leaving the marriage, and through their father's suicide. We became survivors, four distinct people with strong bonds connecting us. Because I always tried to tell them the truth, because their every new independence meant new freedom for me, because we trusted each other even when we wanted different things, they became, at a fairly young age, self-reliant and open to the unfamiliar. Something told me that if they had survived my angers, my self-reproaches, and still trusted my love and each others', they were strong. Their lives have not been, will not be, easy; but their very existences seem a gift to me, their vitality, humour, intelligence, gentleness, love of life, their separate life-currents which here and there stream into my own. I don't know how we made it from their embattled childhood and my embattled motherhood into a mutual recognition of ourselves and each other. Probably that mutual recognition, overlaid by social and traditional circumstance, was always there, from the first gaze between the mother and the infant at the breast. But I do know that for years I believed I should never have been anyone's mother, that because I felt my own needs acutely and often expressed them violently, I was Kali, Medea, the sow that devours her farrow, the unwomanly woman in flight from womanhood, a Nietzschean monster. Even today, rereading old journals, remembering, I feel grief and anger; but their objects are no longer myself and my children. I feel grief at the waste of myself in those years, anger at the mutilation and manipulation of the relationship between mother and child, which is the great original source and experience of love.

On an early spring day in the 1970s, I meet a young woman friend on the street. She has a tiny infant against her breast, in a bright cotton sling; its face is pressed against her blouse, its tiny hand clutches a piece of the cloth. 'How old is she?' I ask. 'Just two weeks old,' the mother tells me. I am amazed to feel in myself a passionate longing to have, once again, such a small, new being clasped against my body. The baby belongs there, curled, suspended asleep between her mother's breasts, as she belonged curled in the womb. The young mother – who already has a three-year-old – speaks of how quickly one forgets the pure pleasure of having this new creature, immaculate, perfect. And I walk away from her drenched with memory, with envy. Yet I know other things: that her life is far from simple; she is a mathematician who now has two children under the age of four; she is living even now in the rhythms of other lives – not only the regular cry of the infant but her three-year-old's needs, her husband's problems. In the building where I live, women are still raising children alone, living day in and day out within their individual family units, doing the laundry, herding the tricycles to the park, waiting for the husbands to come home. There is a babysitting pool and a children's playroom, young fathers push prams on weekends, but childcare is still the individual responsibility of the individual woman. I envy the sensuality of having an infant of two weeks curled against one's breast; I do not envy the turmoil of the elevator full of small children, babies howling in the laundromat, the apartment in winter where pent-up seven- and eight-year-olds have one adult to look to for their frustrations, reassurances, the grounding of their lives.

Mary Lowe
Chasing The Baby

After seven years of trying to conceive, I have finally given up, given in and accepted my fate as a childless woman. And as I sit wondering what the future will bring, I'm pondering over the words: infertile, barren, sterile, 'without issue'. Old-fashioned words that have an almost biblical ring to them, with their connotations of failure, doom and gloom. But before I make myself thoroughly depressed, haven't I forgotten something? Did I not want to be a writer somewhere along the line? What happened to that and all my other dreams? The following is the story of my quest to have a baby and how it has affected my life and writing.

It was like being hooked on drugs, my desire to have a baby. I was addicted, obsessed, it was a habit I needed to feed. Like most drug habits it was great at the beginning. I was infused with hope. My life was planned and I'd been careful: I'd landed myself a job that promised generous maternity provision, a partner who was into the idea, and I had a nice home with a spare bedroom. All I had to do was wait. Every time I saw a baby or a family with children I said to myself, 'Not long now'.

It hadn't always been like that. As a little girl I'd been a tomboy and had never liked dolls. Instead I played football and enjoyed boxing. My hero was Jimmy Cagney, and I was especially drawn to the character he played in *Angels with Dirty Faces*. For a while, as a shy seven-year-old, I developed a swagger and talked tough from the side of my mouth while trying to be morally incorruptible. Babies were boring. They were things that mummies looked after and mummies were boring too. I wanted to be an action hero, hacking my way through jungles. I also loved books and was always reading as a kid. Like many children growing up in the 1960s I was hooked on Enid Blyton's *Famous Five*, *Secret Seven*, *Binkle and Flip* (one of her lesser known works but one of my favourites). I devoured them but it never occurred to me that I might be a writer myself. Writing wasn't a job. Being a writer was akin to being a chest of drawers or a snowman. Completely alien. And as for babies? Nah. I'd visited London Zoo on a school trip and was well impressed: I would be a zoologist, dedicating my life to the care of animals.

It wasn't until adolescence kicked in that I started dreaming about family, husband and home. Call it socialisation, call it brainwashing, me and my friends spent hours talking about our ideal man and poring over mail order catalogues choosing furniture for our imaginary homes. Most of us wanted at least a boy and a girl – I can't remember anyone saying they didn't want a family. My dream was to marry an architect who would be stylish, intelligent and, most important, rich. We would live on a houseboat moored on the Thames and have lots of little children who wore Afghan waistcoats. The fact that my vision of the future bore absolutely no relation to my current life seemed completely immaterial. I was a grammar-school girl and believed that anything was possible provided you were willing to work hard enough. My career ambitions had changed too. I wanted to be a journalist but was already worrying whether I'd be good enough. I knew I could write, I'd written a rash of adolescent poetry and was still interested in words. But being a student had turned books into Literature, writing was for essays, and all the pleasure seemed to have been beaten out of the process.

University was a chance to meet like-minded people, principally men with brains. I settled down in my second year with a lovely boyfriend who was good-looking, charming and interesting. Okay, he wasn't an architect, but he was a Marxist which was more appealing by that stage. Then disaster struck. I was weeks away from the start of my final exams when I discovered I was pregnant. Without thinking too hard about the pros and cons I decided to have an abortion. I was twenty-two, completely broke and involved in a relationship I knew wouldn't last. I went into hospital the day the Falklands War was declared against Argentina: I remember it well as we joked about boycotting the cornbeef sandwiches on the tea menu. While the rest of my friends were revising, I spent three days in hospital writing poems about life, the world, babies. I envisioned him/her sitting on a fluffy pink cloud floating somewhere above my head, curly headed and cute, a kind of cherub. I said goodbye to the cherub and made a promise: I'd have the baby some time in the future, when I was in a better position to care for it. When the ordeal was over (I needed to return twice to hospital, once with an infection and then to have a final D and C), I returned to my books. A few days later I was in my first exam, grappling with questions on later medieval England.

In retrospect, I realise that the pact I'd made in hospital became a central feature of my life for the next twenty years. It served an emotional function – that of coping with my own sense of loss. If I had a child later, I didn't need to mourn the loss of this one; I could get on with the rest of my life without worrying about the consequences. I was a self-determined woman, who'd exercised rights over her own body – such was the rhetoric of the times – and it felt good. So much so that my experience in hospital unleashed a fruitful period of creativity: poems, prose and articles all poured from my pen. I wrote about babies and my own emerging sense of being a woman. Paradoxically, it was a fertile time.

From my mid-twenties onwards, the question of when to have the baby was uppermost in my mind, but as I never had any doubts about my ability to conceive I set about establishing my career first. At this stage I had little time for writing apart from the odd poem, I was too busy doing what you're supposed to do at that age – making a living and enjoying myself. By the time I was thirty I was earning a comfortable salary as a teacher, I had a supportive partner, a network of friends willing to help out with childcare, so I decided to start thinking seriously about pregnancy.

The big change in my life, however, was that I'd become a lesbian, which presented a particular logistic challenge with regard to conception. Lesbians don't just happen to get pregnant; for many of us the decision to have children can mean years of planning.

Getting hold of the sperm is the first hurdle and I learned very quickly that sperm donors do not grow on trees. Many, many men were asked to consider the idea but very few felt positive about it. I talked to friends and friends of friends. I cooked dinners for prospective donors. I constructed questionnaires for interviewing possible candidates. I wrote letters. I was looking for a man who was kind, intelligent and trustworthy. It was a plea from a lonely uterus rather than a lonely heart but the parallels were obvious.

Eventually I plumped for the medical route. A private fertility clinic one hundred and fifty miles away proved to be the nearest place offering treatment to lesbian couples. At that time, 1993, the NHS did not provide donor insemination to lesbians and even now it's virtually impossible to get any kind of fertility treatment (including investigative treatment) through the NHS if you're a lesbian. You have to opt for private medicine which is, of course, expensive. And so began the monthly round of ovulation tests, temperature charts, healthy eating regimes, trips to the clinic and large bills. I had six unsuccessful treatments before I decided to go back to searching for a friendly donor. Eventually one appeared, a friend of a friend who'd already had kids.

Two years down the line I was still trying. I never actually met the man nor knew his name; suffice to say he must have been a pretty laid-back guy to have been willing to do the business month after month. After a year or so I began to feel desperate – I was fast heading towards the age of thirty-five when fertility rates start to plummet, and I knew I had to get a move on. Month after month I clambered back on to the cycle of hope and expectation followed by the crash:

frustration, anger and sadness. At that time I felt that I would never give up. I needed to have this baby and the fact that it was a capricious thing, eluding me at every turn, strengthened my resolve. It became a personal challenge; getting pregnant was akin to winning a gold medal at the Olympics.

I reached a stage when there wasn't room for much else in my life and my creativity reached rock bottom. I found it difficult to write simple reports let alone anything that engaged my imagination. Work went downhill, too – I lost confidence. Now and again I tried to write. I attended an Arvon course and was flattered by positive comments about my work but when I returned home the writing was forgotten.

Eventually, I had to face the fact that the inseminations just weren't working and the process was making me unhappy. So I stopped. There were no fanfares or presents or speeches. I just stopped. I was thirty-seven and a little devilish voice whispered, 'There's still time you can always try again later... But for the moment it was over.

It was time to do something different with my life, and being an impetuous sort of lass, I decided to chuck my job in and buy a round-the-world air ticket. Hey things could be exciting again. I trudged through South-east Asia on my own trying to come to terms with the so-called hole in my life. While travelling I started to feel switched on to things for the first time in ages. My brain seemed to leap into gear. Being surrounded by beauty and excitement helped, of course, and the fact that I was on my own gave me the chance to reflect on what I wanted to do with my life. I saw a world that was at the same time beautiful and depraved stunning and ravished. It was a turning point

I suppose. I wondered about the idea of becoming a writer. Before leaving I'd applied to do an MA in creative writing: what the hell I'd have to fill my life with something and I was pleased to have been offered a place. I knew I wanted to express myself maybe the MA would teach me how.

Returning home six months later, I got a job, started the MA, and simply enjoyed being home with my girlfriend and other friends. But there was still the little voice at the back of my mind nagging 'now or never'...

There was a clinic in Middlesbrough that was offering donor insemination (DI) to lesbians. I knew three women who'd gone there and conceived first time. I decided to check it out. I didn't rush into the decision; I still had the memory of the last stressful phase fresh in my mind. Besides, the more writing I did as a result of the MA, the more committed I became. Writing or Baby? Both were seemingly unattainable goals. I remember writing a poem about my own creativity which turned into a rant against women with children. It described little growth spurts, bubbles of creativity, tiny explosions of colour and language which needed to be tended and listened to before being unleashed into the world. I wanted to dress my poems up and show them off. But who to? Maybe I could be a mother *and* a writer. I'd be forty soon. I knew that time was running out on the baby front.

So back to the grindstone. The clinic was situated on the edge of the North York Moors. The hills surrounding it were beautiful, and the receptionist friendly. Back on the cycle, even though I knew the success rate for DI was low, I naïvely convinced myself that I'd earned this baby and this time I'd be lucky. I convinced myself that whatever happened the outcome would be fine and I'd be cool about it. No stress. If it worked, it worked otherwise, no problem. But just to be on the safe side I'd have acupuncture, any drugs that were offered, possibly go for IVF if necessary.

I declared war against my own infertility. Me and my cheque book against my rapidly ageing eggs.

Is it possible to have fertility treatment and remain halfway human? I tried but I don't think I succeeded. Once again the experience turned into a stressful trip on a medical conveyor belt, involving (unhelpful) GPs, hospitals, blood tests, medicals, injections, swabs, counselling (to ensure that me and my girlfriend weren't axe murderers) – and all that was before we even began the treatment. Over the next year I signed up to an escalating diet of drugs and alternative medicine (acupuncture, reflexology and Chinese herbs). My diary was shot through with stars and numbers: estimated dates of ovulation, actual dates of ovulation, appointments for scans, check ups, pills, injections, inseminations. Despite all my good intentions life had turned one-dimensional again. It was the Chinese herbs that finally tipped me over the edge: boiling up roots and leaves for an hour every other day, to concoct something that looked and tasted like run-off from a chemical plant, made me realise I'd turned into a masochist. I felt as if I was hurling myself against an impenetrable wall, giving myself a battering.

My course work took a dive. Writing stories, poems? I wasn't interested, I didn't have the energy. The stories I did manage to churn out were turgid, leaden. I couldn't concentrate and sat for hours writing and rewriting the same sentence in the hope of getting something right. My mind felt fuzzy, my imagination bound by invisible threads. I blamed it on the tablets. I tried to convince myself that undergoing treatment was creative, that all the misery and deprivation would be worth it in the end.

I stopped writing. For months I could hardly string a sentence together and I deferred my course for a year. I'd had eight treatments spread over eighteen months, a laporoscopy, lots of drugs – God knows how much money I'd poured down the drain. I was sacrificing myself to the idea of a baby, to a hypothetical entity. I realised that I'd been focusing on this one goal for most of the previous decade, yet had nothing to show for it apart from a huge overdraft and a load of misery. It was time to pack it in.

The fear of facing life without children had been one of the reasons I kept trying so hard. Having an abortion and seeking some kind of absolution had deepened my resolve. But when it finally came to it, when I finally said 'I've had enough', all I felt was relief. It was like, 'Aghh, It's over'. My prison sentence. I'd done the time, now I could get on with the rest of my life. When I finally knew it *was* over, it was time to celebrate. I rang up my girlfriend and took her out for a meal.

The experience of trying for a child and failing is exhausting. I thought I was clinging to hope but all the while I was in never-never land. To be creative or artistic requires a certain freedom of thought, an ability to notice, to listen, to play, ultimately to live in the moment for at least some of the time and to be able to capture that moment. I had come to inhabit the world of 'if only', feeding on the fantasy of me with a baby. When I visited bookshops and libraries it had been not for the purpose of browsing fiction but to devour everything they had on infertility. The next stage would have been daily hormone injections and blood tests, spending at least one thousand pounds a month. And after that IVF. I didn't get that far, although I considered it. I know some women will do anything to have a child but I'm thankful that I'm not one of them. But I don't blame them. It's hard not to succumb to the addiction, once you are hooked on the idea of having a baby. As women we are bombarded with images from a very early age teaching us that being female means babies and child rearing. It's quite common for women in my position to say they don't feel like proper women, that something fundamental is missing in their lives. Of course it is. The experience of being a mother is a joyful one for many women. And then there's the question of female bonding. Mothers can talk for hours about kids. It's part of the currency of femaleness and media images reinforce the idea. That's why it's so easy to be borne along by hope on a path constructed by doctors and drug therapy. Every step of the way I said to myself, I've come this far, surely I can't turn back?

Now, a few months into my new childfree existence, I can say that things are looking okay. I look back at the last ten years with some detachment and ask myself the question, what was it all about? Some of it was wanting to have a baby, wanting to be a mother. But not all of it. With hindsight I've recognised other motives, first that of wanting to be accepted as a 'proper woman'. Gay people get dished a lot of low-level criticism that makes us feel invalid, not quite kosher. What better way of buying a bit of acceptance than becoming a mum? I thought I'd gain some brownie points with my parents too, at last they'd be able to relate to me as an adult. Then there was the writing; being a parent would surely present me with all kinds of valuable experience that could be turned into fiction. And the question of leaving something for posterity – the underlying motivation for many artists, wanting to make their mark. But many more people are involved in childrearing than book writing. Why is that? Is it easier? It's certainly a lot more acceptable. And on top of it all was the fear that life without children would be meaningless.

And that's where the writing comes in. There's more space in my head now, it's getting easier. Without children I'll undoubtedly have more time, energy and money. Useful commodities for writers. Those are the positives. Some of the stories I've written relate directly to my experience and the tone of others seems to reflect what I've been feeling. I've written stories on the theme of deception, where characters innocently blunder through a situation that's controlled by someone or something else. I've written about chance. I've not yet written about sadness – somehow that feels too hard at the moment. My writing style tends to be sparky but over the last few months it's turned spiky. I'm angry that I've put ten years of emotional and physical effort into something that hasn't borne fruit when I could have committed the time to writing; I'm angry it's been so much easier for others. But then again...I realise I'm railing against my own destiny.

It wasn't meant to be. My life will take on a different shape. And who knows, perhaps I'll be able to turn my experience into great art. But I have my life back, that's the important thing. And I'm enjoying it.

Julia Alvarez
Imagining Motherhood

Finally, in late fall 1995, my last childless sister became a mother. Forty, single, unlucky in finding a lifelong match, she decided to have a baby on her own. In anticipation of the phone call from the Dominican Republic that would let her know a baby had been found, my sister painted her spare bedroom a soft lavender; she went shopping for baby clothes; she considered a dozen names and heard feedback on possible awful nicknames that might come of them; she baby-proofed her house. And she talked and talked and talked about the upcoming baby.

Every time she'd start in, I'd feel my chest tightening. Pushing its thorny head through the veneer of cheeriness and encouragement was that old monster all sisters are well acquainted with: jealousy. It was like being back in childhood, in the full of summer, with my sister anticipating her big birthday party in July while mine had already gone by way back in March.

My other two sisters had raised their babies in a flurry of diapers and photo albums full of the cute little critters. That was back in my early thirties. I loved my niece and nephews to bits. I uncurled their tiny infant hands, smelled their baby powder skin, wrote them poems on every occasion, but I was glad to hand them over at the end of the visit and get back to my writing.

You mean they didn't stop howling like that when you wanted to finish a chapter? They had to be driven to what? Suzuki recorder lessons, just when your editor called with a request you had to mail out that night? No, thanks. I'd gladly be the godmother, sending birthday cheques and little gifts, but as for being the good mother, well, I just didn't have the time.

Then suddenly mid-forty, I realised what most of my women friends must have realised in high school. We *are* mortal. We don't have an endless supply of time. By now, I'd already used up half of mine or more, and I had only a couple of years left if I truly wanted a child. I could always adopt, but I had to make up my mind soon or I'd be following that poor kid to school on my walker, for heaven's sake.

But it was more than a biological clock that was ticking away; it was a familial one as well. In my family of four sisters, two and two is a fine balance, but if three sisters go a certain route, the fourth sister can't bear the loneliness and caves in to the majority choice. It's the old story of women living together in a house: their menstrual periods will eventually synchronise.

With us, it went further – we all got married within the space of a few years, at least the first time around. Overnight, we all had the same sensible short haircut because our 1960s manes were just too hard to keep up (and made us look passé). Then, we all seemed to find silk one Christmas, shimmering loose outfits that freed us to move without constraints (no funny bras safety-pinned to things we had to be careful not to tear, no tight waistlines reminding us that we were eating too much of Mami's flan de guayaba). Only two stayed in long-term marriages, leaving the other two to commiserate over the dearth of good middle-aged men.

Then last November, my compañera in childlessness, my baby sister and fellow maverick, became a mami. When she called from the Dominican Republic with the news, I burst into tears. 'I'm so...happy,' I sobbed, 'so, so happy.'

And I was. Who wouldn't be? To have my beautiful niece suddenly bringing up the rear of the next generation of our family! Had any child ever been so cute! I mean, Benetton babies, beware! I went through my town, showing off photos. On the way home, it struck me that I was acting as if I were the proud mother. But it was my sister's birthday party. Again, I burst into tears.

'Nothing in the world compares to this, nothing,' my sister kept saying. I finally asked her to please stop saying so, please.

Because the yearning hit strong. Suddenly, I noticed there were babies everywhere. Every junior colleague had a babe in her arms – and these moms were getting their writing done as well. How did younger women learn to do that? As for my women friends – those old-world fems, as these younger women now refer to us – my 'old' friends were suddenly busy with babies, too. Most of them, having reared their children, had joined me in our knockabout middle years, their empty nests looking a whole lot like my one-person one. But now they were becoming grandmothers of beautiful grandbabies they couldn't stop talking about.

By this time, I had remarried, but alas, my husband's two daughters were grown girls I couldn't sit on my knee and cuddle. So, of course, the question came up: Why not have or adopt our very own child?

'What do you think?' I kept asking Bill.

His face would get a stricken look. He had already raised his babies, and though it was worth (almost) every minute of it, he didn't want to start all over again at fifty. He was at the stage I was in my late twenties and thirties when I wanted to give those pooping, wailing babies back to their mothers.

But hearing my tearful plaints month after month, he finally caved in. 'If it's something you really think you have to have, I'll do it for you.'

With the choice presented in terms of what *only* I wanted, the same indecisiveness struck again. Oh, I knew Bill would rally one hundred per cent to become a father. Still, hadn't I been inside marriages where my life's direction was dictated by a partner's passion, not my own? How long and dreary that road can become! And at our age – a phrase I find myself saying more and more – there just isn't time to be taking too many tangents away from where we have left to go.

But my decision was not ultimately a submission to Bill's preference. I had to face the fact that it had been my own choice not to become a mother. The thought of putting aside – even for just a few years – what I had always considered my real calling, the writing, putting it aside now in my mid-forties when I was finally hitting my full stride, gave me cold feet. I came to realise with that straight, clear eyed vision of a writer analysing her fictional characters that I didn't really want to be a mother solely for the sake of being a mother.

Yet I still felt the pressure to at least say I wanted to be a mother. For all our talk of feminism and pro-choice, wilful childlessness continues to have a bad reputation. That Victorian view of childless women as not fully realised lingers. A woman who doesn't care to have a child is considered foolish at best. At worst, as I heard one lecturer proclaim, she is 'committing genetic suicide'.

Among my friends and acquaintances here in rural Vermont, the rearing, educating and taking care of children has been a major focus of their lives. 'You're lucky,' they tell me, but beyond a momentary weariness, what I hear in their voices is a secret pride at the fecundity of their lives.

And if being childless is unusual in rural Vermont, it is *mucho más* odd in my own Latin culture, where being a woman and a mother arc practically synonymous. Being childless – by choice – is tantamount to being wicked and selfish. Marriage is a sacrament for the procreation of children, how many times have my old *t'as* told me that? Even the one family holdout, my maiden aunt who grew orchids and read books and knew Latin, finally married in her thirties and had her one child. 'I won't deny,' she has told me, 'that this has been the most significant event of my life.'

Ever since I married Bill, the pressure has mounted. On my annual visit to the Island, the inevitable question pops up, Don't I want a child? More tactful aunts approach the topic through my eating habits. Don't I know I have to put aside that vegetarian foolishness in order to strengthen my body for a child. 'But you have to have your *niño*,' my aunt's maid told me. It's mandatory, she might as well have said. Last year, when my sister adopted, I almost cancelled my trip.

'That'll make you feel even worse,' my husband wisely counselled. He was right.

The only way to come to terms with the yearning was to accept that it was a loss. Just as never having learned a musical instrument or never having become a bullfighter or a ballerina is a loss. As is never having grown up in the Dominican Republic amid my own people; never having learned the languages to read Dante, Tolstoy, Rilke in the original. All these are losses now – instead of possibilities to be left open – because I know that given my age, there isn't time enough for all that I once meant to do with my life. You can't have everything, our mothers used to tell us. So why *is* it that our me-generation tends to feel cheated if we can't have everything? Maybe part of accepting childlessness is accepting this rude fact.

But in accepting my chosen loss, I've come to realise that, ironically, I was grieving over the loss to my writing more than anything else. A good part of my sudden, last-minute reconsideration of motherhood has sprung from a writer's approach to life: I do not want to miss out on a valuable experience that might help me to understand people better, that might inform my spirit and intelligence, make me a better human being, and (dare I say it?) a better writer.

As my best woman friend, thrice a mother, and recently a new grandmother reminds me: What is the imagination for if everything requires life experience? She's right. I can imagine motherhood. I don't need to subject a child to my writerly personal growth experience, if that's what I'm after. Spare the poor kid a grandmother-mother who wears dentures. (I can just imagine a whole new category of your mamma-wears-army-boots jokes!) Now, when I travel to my native Dominican Republic, and my *tías* inquire after my sister and her new baby, and winking at Bill, ask us if we don't feel inspired, I will have to say, 'Yes, I feel inspired.' Inspired, that is, to come home and write about it.

Nicole Ward Jouve
Learning to Mother Myself

I wrote my first novel when my first child was a few months old. The novel was called *Je, me, moi*. Which might be mistranslated as 'me, me, me'. It now seems to speak volumes that I should have chosen such a title: was I asserting my right to individual existence in the face of marriage and motherhood? The novel certainly had nothing to do with either.

I remember the writing itself, indeed the whole period, as blissfully happy. We were renting a cottage (Rose Cottage if you please), in a village not far from York where both my husband and I were teaching. I had a part-time job, very part-time. On the days when I had classes, kindly, motherly Mrs Porter took excellent care of my son. It was spring. On the days when I stayed at home, I put my son out in the garden in his pram under the apple tree. Hopeful of worms, perhaps, a robin would perch on the upright handle of a spade, which stood forgotten in the earth. The robin would cock its head and wonder. The weather was, somehow, always fine. I sat at the kitchen table, at a window facing the garden, and wrote. When the baby started to cry I would bring him in and feed him. Sometimes I'd go and check. He was watching the sky, the boughs, the flitting birds. The wonder of it all.

My novel took place in Italy, by the sea. My heroine was wicked, and her wickedness gave me great pleasure. Somehow the writing got steeped in clear English spring light, apple blossoms, the pliant grass, what was left of the leeks in the tiny vegetable patch, gypsy women calling one morning to sell pegs. I showered them with gifts because every time I bought or gave them something ('You don't happen to have any tea to spare, dearie?', 'Clothes or shoes to spare, dearie?') they bestowed 'a thousand blessings' on the little one.

Then things changed. My son began to crawl, then walk. He had to be watched. Another baby was on its way. I got more teaching, then a fulltime job. We moved to an isolated house, and my world collapsed with the disappearance of Mrs Porter. Babysitters were like gold dust: hard to find. We moved to a flat in town. It seemed to rain perpetually. There was a disastrous series of home-helps, from one who was accident prone and worked two and a half days in three weeks before she quit, to one who moved into our flat with all her brood when we were away at weekends. I was always tired. Teaching, reading, marking, shopping, cooking, washing up, tidying up, cleaning, changing babies, dealing with fights, measles, visitors and the ever-overgrown garden. The world was all demands, and I was supposed to satisfy them. I had a mild dose of postnatal depression. The children caught every childhood illness that was around, and the home-help phoned in sick every time I had an early morning class. I broke my ankle. A third baby was on its way. After work, I would catch a bus on my crutches, collect the children from nursery school, shop with the shopping bag around my neck. Leisure time? Don't make me laugh. It was a dream of the past. No question of writing. Even my diary became an outpouring of despair. 'Me me me' cried in her cot: she was left unheard and starving in her stinking, soaked nappies.

I only understood this years later – that there is a little child in us that needs tending – once age had restored the luxury of leisure time.

No wonder that when in the early 1970s, I became aware of the feminist movement burgeoning all around me, I was most drawn to writers like Adrienne Rich or Tillie Olsen who questioned motherhood. How do you create if you are a mother? Aren't children supposed to be your creation? Reproduction it is called: tell someone else. Bloody hard work if you ask me. How do you reconcile the demands of children, which are immediate, with the demands of creation? Something pulls at you from inside, demanding concentration, silence, time. Delicate, impatient of interruption. Children pull at you from the outside, demanding attention, food, care. Children need love, tolerance, patience. Writing, to be powerful and complete, requires boldness, total commitment, cruelty. It abhors compromise. Or so I felt.

Things eased up. There was a marked improvement when my youngest started school. I had found a good childminder, who lived in the village we had moved to. I wrote the stories that went to make up *Le Spectre du gris – Shades of Grey* in the English translation. Editions des Femmes published it in France; Virago in England. Each of the stories was a protest – against the inhumanity of a maternity hospital that treated mothers and infants as things to be processed, not as people; against marriage and motherhood such as my generation had experienced them. Most of the couples in those stories were unhappy. Much of it was the man's fault. The women were desperate to be mothers. One died of the accumulated frustration and grief of being childless. But most were run into the ground by the children's exuberant and greedy presence. Was motherhood incompatible with creating?

I had several arguments about this with a friend who is a sculptor. She has four children, one of whom is, in her words, 'severely handicapped'. She also had a part-time teaching job but at no point, did she say that her children were a hindrance to her creativity. She stopped when she had to and could always start whenever there was a bit of time. As she was assuring me, I suspected that she was speaking out of loyalty to, and fondness for, her children, especially the disabled daughter. But maybe I was wrong. Maybe with sculpture there are lots of practical, physical jobs that you can start and stop; that don't demand utter concentration, as writing does. Or maybe she just was a good, naturally loving and competent mother. I feel I was not; mothering did not come easy to me. I had to work at it. I wanted a Mrs Porter around, to mother *me* as she mothered my children. Not that I did not love my children with all my heart, but I wanted some time to myself. Unconsciously, sometimes consciously, I resented them. Perhaps hated them? I have been told that with postnatal depression vulnerable mothers turn their hatred of their offspring or of the total, unbearable demand being made on them into self-hatred in order to protect their children. That would fit. I was both fragile and selfish. Such was the judgement I passed on myself.

On the other hand, my friend thought it was husbands who prevented a woman from being an artist, although her husband had never stopped her.

(Not been able to, I thought to myself.) But she had two very gifted friends, both painters, both mothers, whose husbands, also artists, had not tolerated that they be artists too. The friends had caved in and had let their great talents go to waste.

There are many such stories in my generation and the preceding generations – women whose creativity has been stifled by the complex demands of domesticity, the difficulties of combining the traditional roles of wife and mother with the new ones of having a career, and being the other or sole breadwinner. And, with changing gender roles, there are now also men whose family responsibilities have prevented them from being the creators they would like to be, just as Alton Locke and Jude the Obscure were debarred by class from giving form to their vision. Not that class disadvantages or living in severely deprived areas of the world don't continue to choke or impede creativity today. Yet these things are paradoxical, as are most things: sometimes out of oppression or material deprivation, great creativity is born (I am thinking here of Tsitsi Dangarembga's *Nervous Conditions*).

I think of the great creators of the past – Dante, Michelangelo, da Vinci, Shakespeare, Beethoven – and wonder: did they have anything else to do but write, sculpt, paint, make music? Was there anything in their lives to stop them from giving themselves to their heart's passion? Even on a more modest scale, Virginia Woolf's demand for 'a room of one's own' and 'two hundred pounds a year' (or today's equivalent) for a woman to be able to create rings true. How about the money required to pay a good and reliable babysitter? Mothering was not something

Woolf considered as part of the equation. Given the cost to her of birthing her novels, the sheer exhaustion and sometimes breakdown that followed completion, it is impossible to imagine her caring for children as well. In her case it was clearly either/or. Perhaps, if one aims at greatness, it has to be either/or.

And yet, if I look at my own relation to motherhood and creativity – now that, in the late and last part of my life I have no one to care for but myself – I have more than the symbolic two hundred, and more than one room of my own. Now that I am totally free – that I only need to clean if I am minded to do so, or cook for others if the fancy takes me, now that I could stay in bed for ever, like the decadent nineteenth-century Russian aristocrat Oblomov, now that I could go and live on top of a mountain, spend a year, two years there, writing one of those books I dreamed of writing and never had time for when I was young – how differently I view all this. I note that I manage to keep extraordinarily busy, so that writing remains something I salvage time for in the face of great pressure – however absurd or self-created that pressure might be. Duties to others, often imaginary, take precedence over my own work. Have I become addicted to being busy and feeling harassed? Am I afraid to let go of a mode of being that is now obsolete or is this a form of co-dependency making me feel important? Am I afraid of solitude, of facing up to myself; of not being needed, when what gave me an identity for so long was to be in permanent demand?

One of my friends, due to retire and with adult children like myself, had a breakdown. She was in and out of hospital for three years. 'I existed because I was a mother and a teacher,' she said to me. 'Now I am nothing.' She keeps afloat by creating a timetable of charitable duties that fills up her week the way teaching did. Weekends are a problem. Perhaps I am doing the same, but in a more self-indulgent way.

And this opens the question: was it motherhood that was in the way of my creativity when I was a young woman, or was it *me*? There is no doubt that the sheer labour of mothering takes time and energy but does it really have to be the battle I experienced? I have my doubts.

I suddenly feel very grateful that I've been asked to write this piece. For it enables me to see something – the way I create pressure for myself; the way in which I only seem able to write in the midst of pressure, at stolen moments. Perhaps this is something I can change. That way lies true freedom ...

It also makes me see that my attitudes to motherhood and creativity *have* changed. It is one of the blessings of age, that things keep evolving, that one keeps growing, while in other ways one is waning. Motherhood – or mothering – now seems such an extraordinary privilege and is one I feel deeply grateful for. This is what I would like to share with readers. This may be what I can contribute to the question.

Everything had to do with 'me, me, me'.

Ten years ago my life came crashing down. My props collapsed – people close to me had breakdowns, became depressed, suicidal, died. My own career took a nosedive. All at once I came to feel that I had failed in everything I had hoped to be good at: motherhood and creativity among them. I went into analysis, which is one of the things that saved my sanity. In time, a number of things began to look very different.

All my life I had mistaken the ideal for the real. I had dreamed of being a perfect wife and mother, a great writer. I believe this all stems from the way children are brought up to be good. Not just good, very good, because that was what won approval, and love. Even God only loved you if you were good. Okay, Jesus said he had come to save sinners, but that was just his way of being kind. In any case, boy, didn't you just sin all the time! What you had to do was control your own badness and work at being good. No one ever added, 'at everything', but I was ambitious! You name it, I wanted it.

I was possessed, as a friend now puts it, by the 'demon of comparison'. I was going to be Saint Teresa, Rita Hayworth, Cathy from *Wuthering Heights*, Florence Nightingale, George Sand and Julie Andrews rolled into one. If somebody was good at something, I was going to be better. It was my understanding that if you didn't achieve your goals, it was your own fault. You just had to try harder.

That was how I had been brought up. I no longer feel resentful of my parents or grandparents as that was how they'd been brought up too. My mother lost her father when she was eight. On his deathbed he said to her: 'Be very good.' She dedicated her life to this. I was lucky: I escaped, married out of my class and country, and chose a man who had no intention of being good at all. I had rebelled in the best way I could.

As a mother I tried very hard. I did all that the (medical and educational) authorities of my day prescribed. I kept the home fires burning: made jams, pickles, chutneys, soft toys, lampshades, curtains, cushions. I baked, picked berries, sewed, knitted, crocheted, went to auction sales, stripped pine furniture, told stories in bed (it took over six happy months to read our way through *Lord of the Rings*). There was fun, there was joy, even comfort along the way. But deep down something was wrong: the untended child from way back kept crying 'me, me, me'.

I became over-sensitive, anxious, driven by this passion or that. I felt I lacked the resources to mother. In the frenzy of well-meaning activity, blinded by my own unfelt needs, ratty with exhaustion or in bed with migraine, I missed the things that mattered, mishandled situations and failed to see what my children's real problems were. Years later I understood. Like Miss Havisham in *Great Expectations* I cried 'What have I done?'

In one of her angry periods my daughter said to me, 'You wanted your own children to mother you.' She was right, and I was ashamed. I desperately needed to be cared for, I who consciously wanted to care for others. Something in me cried out, 'Please help me,' and it was at my children's expense. I was brittle. As a child I had never got recognition for who I really was – the mixture of good and bad that was me. Because I was expected to be good, there was nowhere for the bad to go, which is why writing was such a lifeline. When I wrote I could be bad and it gave me balance.

It took a long time to discover the needy child, the passionately angry little girl deep down inside me. It also took a long time to begin to rebuild relations with my parents and my children. What I wanted was forgiveness for myself, who did the best I could, and for those I resented or was angry at. It has been a long haul, but it has come.

I am neither a great mother nor a great writer nor a great human being. I was certainly not a great wife. I shall never be Mother Teresa or Virginia Woolf. But I am what I am, and that is okay. I still disappoint myself and smart from the disappointment. But then I remember what there is to love and in doing so, I learn to mother myself. When I manage to love myself, there always comes a rush of gratitude, peace and joy and as I learn to love myself, I note that I care more for others.

I remember Thomas Hardy. The Mayor of Casterbridge ends up thinking that when we have the power, we do not have the knowledge, and when we have the knowledge, we no longer have the power. It is a truthful, but also a blinkered thing to say. For we only have real knowledge when we have it in our hearts, and what is in the heart is never lost. There is a mother in us – men as well as women – which, when it comes into being, gives us both the love that we need and the capacity to love others. There is an ability to mother which is what makes us truly creative.

The sun is shining today. It is the first day of spring. Instead of cleaning, shopping, answering mail or marking, I will go out and watch the unfurling, soft green buds of the chestnut trees in the Luxembourg gardens. That will be my way of mothering myself. Of being creative.

Tomorrow I may choose to write.

Ellen Bell
The Sixth Swan

Last night I dreamed that I was changing my baby daughter's nappy. She was as slippery as an eel, wet and giggling. Every time I managed to get the nappy under her writhing bottom, the tapes at the side would not stick down. With tears of frustration rolling down my cheeks I finally gave in and let her scramble down off the bed, triumphant and nappyless. I was awoken by the alarm clock seconds later, and a cloying consciousness of failure remained with me.

For some it would be shrugged off as a mere dream, whereas I know it to be a metaphor for my brief encounter with motherhood. My daughter will soon be a teenager, but my memories of looking after her remain frozen at the time when she was barely two years old.

A delicious, though daunting, sense of the inevitability that I was to be an artist was just beginning to take root the year that I became pregnant. I had come to London as a cautious nineteen-year-old to study theatre design. I was a willing sponge but a slow reactor. With my degree over and a creative persona barely formed, I chose to travel for a year, putting off decisions that I did not have the sagacity to make.

Three years of the kind of 'this and that', which appears to be a prerequisite of the artist's apprenticeship, followed. Bit by bit opportunities came forward and I took them, hungrily. In hindsight, I can see that I was too hungry. I never fully weighed up the consequences before rushing headlong into whatever came my way. I think this has something to do with never feeling quite good enough. And when one doesn't feel quite good enough, one ends up believing that one is a fraud. I had waded into the deep end without truly trusting my ability to swim.

I was working as a model maker, acquiring new skills and excited by the environment that I found myself in. Deep down, however, I was growing scared. Scared that my fraudulent self would emerge and I would fail to live up to the expectations of my new employers. It is almost as if I became pregnant at the point when I gave up on my own potential.

The period of time between discovering that I was pregnant and giving birth to my child remains indistinct. I felt like I had woken up in another country. I was no longer in charge. Decisions were made about me and for me, without anyone really asking for my opinion. In a spirit of panic, the father of my child and I decided to get married. It was a clumsy affair and belonged to someone else's life, not mine. The road had narrowed and I had no option but to keep moving forward. Forward towards the event that had brought these two virtual strangers together in matrimony.

It was a difficult time. We decided to move north in the hope of finding work and more affordable accommodation but it was the wrong decision. My husband found work but I couldn't. Our home was one room at the top of a rented house and the only consolation was an enormous bathtub sunk into the floor of our room. I would spend hours lying in the tub contemplating my growing belly, almost in a trance. I had begun to draw again, my own body mostly. It fascinated me, alien yet familiar. I would watch with interest the changes that were taking place. The dark brown line from my belly button downwards appeared like a lovingly etched scar. And my breasts intrigued me too. They had become full and ripe, yet no longer seemed to be sexual. These quiet periods are all that I can really remember from that time. The birth came quickly and I, as mother, was born.

It is tricky for me to separate my struggles with learning to mother from my struggles with learning to create. Mostly, they were indivisible. Inside I hadn't stopped being me; the me that wanted – no, needed – to create something that was her own. And yet, outside my work, my living activity had become mothering. Looking back I suspect that I suffered from a degree of postnatal depression, or perhaps I was just desperately unhappy.

She was a long, big, healthy and extremely hungry baby and feeding her was an endless activity. She, and my misery, drank me dry within a couple of months.

When I succumbed to the loving of her there were moments of peace, a gentle acquiescence. But our life was too fraught with uncertainty for this to last. We moved again and again. In one year we moved over ten times, never into a proper home, usually staying with friends who were kind enough to shelter us. I was a mess. My very essence was being eroded. I desperately wanted to stand still, be conscious and yet not have to be responsive, in any way, to another being.

We ended up on the south coast, renting a small flat above an Indian restaurant. My husband had found work in London and consequently lived there during the week. I alone was responsible for our baby, five days out of seven. Day and night. I was lonely and withdrawn. My waking hours were filled with caring for her. The flat was cold, so I took her into the bed with me. She was a self-contained baby, robust and vigorous, yet undemanding in a way. It was almost as if she sensed that I wasn't truly awake. The only drawings that I did during that time were tiny, overworked sketches of her asleep. It seems to me these clumsy drawings say more of my condition at that time than hers.

From our brief resting place by the sea we went abroad towards a promise of work for me. For a time all was well. That is, I was working and creating, while my husband took over the daily care of our daughter. The work I was producing was not to my own design but I had a say in its conception, which was something. This new start was short-lived, however, and within a couple of months the work had dried up. Soon, all the walls came tumbling down. The marriage was over. I returned to England with my daughter, jobless and homeless. My family gave us shelter for a while, but I knew that their patience would soon run out. Eventually we found a room to let in a family's house. They were very kind and welcoming. My daughter was thrilled to be among a body of friendly faces and very quickly settled in; however, nothing had been solved – we had somewhere to live for the time being, but that was all.

I believe that it was the need somehow to find my way back to what I had been, or at least thought I could be, that prompted me to leave her. I desperately needed to be alone. No, not alone – I needed not to be a mother. It would just be for a little while, I told myself. So I left her. She was safe, living where we had lived together as fugitives from another life. But she was no longer a fugitive; she belonged, whereas I did not. She was eighteen months old when I caught the train for London. And she was home for the first time in her life. She had her own bedroom. She attended a day nursery She was loved. She was happy.

My cancellation of myself as mother was a painful process. Sitting on that train, watching the northern landscape drain away, I couldn't make sense of what I was feeling. I was numb. But somewhere deep inside I knew that I had committed an act that would form my persona from that day forward. Leaving my child was both the birth and death of myself. The dying came first and then the mourning. I missed her madly. I yearned, longed and ached for her. It was a primal longing, silent howling late into the night. Amid this inner turmoil I managed to cobble together something that looked like a life. I found work and a place to live. I shared a flat with a dear friend who showed tireless patience in listening to my endless stream of guilt and self-deprecation. And, for the first time in over two years I found time to be alone.

I would spend my free time wandering around the city, visiting galleries, public spaces and a variety of cafés. I began to sketch what I saw. It was therapeutic and took me out of my own particular quagmire. At times, I even forgot myself and the longing I felt for my daughter.

I stayed in London for two years. I was drawing regularly by then and had a strong portfolio of work so when I attended my interview for the Illustration degree course at Manchester Polytechnic, I was accepted. Five years have passed since I completed my last degree, and my work, like myself, has changed greatly. Leaving my daughter ten years ago has defined the way I live and the art that I create. Writing this brief account of my life has helped me to see this and has been a strangely cathartic process, ironing out many of the creases that have long been overlooked. It has also forced me to question the importance of my work, to define it in simple terms, unsentimentally.

Essentially, my art, my work, represents my inner life. I was completely unable to sustain this inner life while being a mother to my child. I am not denying any responsibility for my failings over this; I didn't know how to be a mother. I didn't know how to make it work both for her and for me. Caring for her meant there was nothing left of me, for me. There have been countless analogies made between giving birth and making art. One can understand why. The expectation, the hoping, the nurturing, the screaming, the pain and the exhilaration. For me, it is also the mess that is the same. The bloody goo between one's legs as this slimy creature spills out, sprawling and coughing. The mixture of fear and wonder at its creation. And most of all, your part in it. That is the most wondrous thing of all. This creature, this tiny pup, has come into your world and it needs you to form, to nurture and feed it.

Making art, whether it be good or bad, strident or intimate, needs time – time to fail, to experiment and to make journeys. To make art one needs a robust spirit, or, failing that, a willing one. Making art needs energy. I believe that to be a mother the requirements are the same. So how does one split oneself, especially if one has this need to do both well? Certainly in my life I couldn't find the answer.

I suspect that I have paid for my decision to run from this quandary, and there are often times when I feel like the youngest brother in the tale of 'The Six Swans'. His sister doesn't have time to finish the left sleeve of his shirt, so he must spend the rest of his life with a wing for an arm. (As a child I often used to wonder how he fared.) Of course I am not alone in this disfigurement, for my daughter too will no doubt feel marred by what her mother did to her. When we meet or speak on the phone, I do my best to respond to her questions honestly, but I am aware of the onus I carry.

Motherhood exposes women to extremes of sensations and emotions. At times I felt as if my flesh had been stripped off. So exposed, so in love, so frightened for that tender being for whom I was responsible. I wanted to run from such powerful feelings from the very start. They overwhelmed me.

Creating can expose you to similar sensations. It is a messy business making art: one is forced to show one's beginnings, knickerless and tripping. And yet one must do it. Though I have never truly considered myself to be a good artist, I have always felt that I had no choice but to continue being one.

Much of my work is deeply rooted in traditional fairy tales. They are mostly familiar stories, like those written by Charles Perrault, Hans Christian Andersen and collected by the Brothers Grimm. For me these tales reveal the duality of existence in a refreshing, matter-of-fact way. The brutal and the gentle mingle and learn from each other. And all creatures are welcome: black or white, hairy or bald, thin or fat, big or small. These stories are about balance.

Metamorphosis or shape-shifting are popular themes within the tales, often involving a female protagonist. Girls are set impossible tasks, usually domestic in nature, that they must fulfil to enable them to pass through into their new form or existence. The power of speech is frequently taken from them during the test, so their endurance, their pain and their fear must be borne silently. As a girl I was deeply moved by the mute sufferings of these young women in stories like 'The Handless Maiden', 'Rapunzel' and 'The Six Swans'. They bore their fate with fortitude and courage. Of course, as an adult, I can hear the hushed moral tone of the storyteller, passing on his or her cultural ideal of womanhood. These tales were a subtle form of correction. I can see that. But even so, such women formed my childish idea of what was right. I use these tales now as starting points for my own personal statements, they set the scene. They allow me to climb inside my own 'donkeyskin' and speak through my experience of the forbidden 'red shoes'.

Many tales comment on tensions within families. There are the common stereotypes of ineffectual fathers, brutal stepmothers, and absent or dead natural mothers. They reflect the familial difficulties of their time while still being relevant today. My own parents' marriage was not a happy one. As children my sisters and I withdrew into ourselves. Being witness to my mother's bitter disappointment made me determined to carve out something different for myself. The only problem was I lacked a real role model so I didn't really know how things could be different. I had absorbed the fairy tales' strictures of silence, endurance and hard work, but many years would pass before I truly understood the process and reward involved in passing that ultimate test.

And there are rewards. Ten years on, I am living a completely new life. I have a room of my own to work in and because I have the support, both emotional and financial, of my partner, I am able to make art that satisfies me. Though I have again chosen to live with someone, I believe that I am essentially a solitary person. Much of my work is played out in my head during times of solitude. When I am alone it is as if I forget my outer self, my age, my sex, even my identity. I am a kind of medium through which the work evolves and I need to create a barrier against the real world to effect this.

The love that my new husband gives me has made an incredible difference to my creative life. The same high expectations of myself as a mother that helped convince me my daughter would be better off without me eject me just as harshly from my studio. But now I have someone who listens to my fears and counterbalances them, before lovingly returning me to myself. Perhaps, if I had been offered a similar framework of support in my earlier uncertainty, then it might have been possible to balance my needs as a mother and an artist.

When I first left my daughter and went to London I kept her existence to myself. She was my secret. I was scared that people would judge me as harshly as I was judging myself. Even now I am wary of revealing her existence. There is a part of me that believes that this is terrible, as if I am somehow denying her room in my world. Perhaps I am.

Though I maintain regular contact with her by letter and phone, and she visits me every year, our relationship has had to be reconstructed, almost from scratch. The mothering of her is being fulfilled by another and I must take a secondary role. That role is a strange one, unfamiliar and uncomfortable. But I must, and do, accept it.

Two years ago, I agreed to participate in a film about errant mothers. I agonised over my decision, however, uncertain about what such exposure would bring. It was an emotionally charged experience. But in the end I believe I did it for the right reasons: for me, and for others like me.

My original conception of motherhood was that it was self-annihilating. I have since met women for whom it is both a joy and a challenge. I stand in awe of them. I like to believe that there are women out there whose spirits are big and brave enough to form a fulfilling life for themselves as well as for their children. Perhaps we need to be exposed to such a life as children first, to be able to perpetuate a similar one for ourselves.

I find that it is virtually impossible to close this inner debate with any kind of certainty. Motherhood and creativity are both honourable ways of living. Both can be altruistic, or self-centred. Both are hard to inflict boundaries upon. Unless one has outside support both can take over one's life. Both can even be the cause for ending it.

I haven't solved the problem. I am still a mother, albeit an absent one. I made a decision that I feel was the right one for her and for me. In no way am I advocating that one should leave one's child for the sake of one's art. For me it was the only way forward for both of us, that's all. In the tale of 'The Handless Maiden' the girl has her hands chopped off because she refuses to marry the devil. After many trials and sorrows, she eventually finds love and security and slowly, very slowly, her hands grow back. Mine are almost there.

Sue Woolfe
Calculating the Madonna

Before I started writing, in fact for all my childhood, I had the impression that writers were special people, Moses-like characters, men – because in my childhood the only people who seemed to have the right to speak universally, disinterestedly and sexually neutrally were men.[1] This was despite the obvious presence of women writers. I even assumed Harriet Beecher Stowe was a man, her name being a funny American variation on Harry. So, writers were privileged men who ascended somewhere, up into the haze, and there received the idea for a novel. This impression was not dispelled by my undergraduate and postgraduate courses in English literature. No one in all those years of study ever thought to mention that the novel is, as a fellow writer said to me the other day, a very messy medium. I've often wondered why they didn't mention it. Perhaps they didn't care.

So when I at last dared to think I might be ready to write a novel, I went for luck up to the top of a mountain in Greece and prepared to receive the vision. But the process that evolved was so messy, so ramshackle and drifting and meandering, so full of muddle and mis-starts, that I was constantly plunged into shame. No real writer, I blushed, would work like this.

Let me explain. The way I work seems to be connected with the configuration of my house, I write my early draft by hand, usually upstairs in the attic. Downstairs there's a dining room and off that is a study. I don't normally have such luxurious space to myself, but at that time particular circumstances made it possible. Upstairs, I was writing a novel about an amateur woman mathematician who has discovered a new sort of number, but because she is outside the mathematics establishment, she can't tell anyone who'll understand her. This novel seemed to be coming together in a very meandering way. Downstairs, on the computer because I thought it was in its last draft, was a factual diary of my first year with my baby.

Because everyone in my life would be a lot happier if I actually completed something, I felt I ought to work on the diary. I was only a few weeks off sending it out to a publisher, but something was wrong. The easiest way to explain what was wrong is to say it wasn't a story. It didn't have any symbolic power or cartwheel off into many directions – it was a mere compilation of factual events and to me facts have always seemed an evasion. Then I read something by my friend Patti Miller and it set my heart cartwheeling:

If I could be held up to the light, it would shine through me in a strange dappled pattern; and looking closer you would see I was made of densely woven stories which blocked and let through the light in this intricate way... I want to find out what these stories are, where they have come from, and what they are making of me. I suspect they influence, if not control, my small daily actions, my friends, my passions, fears and journeys.

So I held myself up to the light.

I have to explain something else personal – I'm a very bewildered mother. Well-meaning, but bewildered. And when I held myself up to the light for the stories of bewildered mothers, I found something totally unexpected. I found a gap. An empty space. I panicked. After a lifetime of reading, why this gap? I needed these stories because like Patti Miller, stories, by some complex system of comparison and congruence, tell me who I am.

I could see many stories of mothers who are reliable, dependable, courageous, who battle for their children, who are martyred for their children... mothers who are the equivalent of girls on a school hockey team determined to win the match for the good of all. But that wasn't what I was looking for. I was looking for stories about mothers a bit like me. I could also see stories about mothers who are destructive and malevolent. Usually they are step-mothers as if a natural mother could never never be unkind, fickle, skittish, bad-tempered, or blundering. Only these two extremes: good or evil.

In few of the stories are mothers well-meaning but ramshackle. They're seldom self-absorbed and narcissistic with moments of personal grandeur that have nothing to do with nurturing. They're seldom idealistic failures – in fact, they seldom have complex ideals at all, beyond the one true ideal of their children's good. And if they are more complex, such as Anna in *The Good Mother* by Sue Miller, where Anna, a single mother, tries to explore her sexuality, they still almost always find their real self-fulfilment in nurturing.

I wanted stories about mothers who don't find their real self-fulfilment in nurturing. I wanted stories about a woman who is, for example, passionate about her work outside the home; stories that explore the struggles and compromises she has to make in her professional life when her babies are born, whether she grieves for the loss of her ambitions, whether it hurts to put them on hold, indeed, whether she *has* to put them on hold, and whether it ultimately destroys her. Stories about a woman who has never had a professional life, but needs one.

All my life I'd read stories about the effect of a mother on her children but what about the effect of the children on the mother: mother-centred stories? I wondered whether the effect of having a baby was exclusively to domesticate a woman. I could see that it could also make a mother more passionate, more creative in her work outside the home in a way that has nothing to do with her children. It could deepen her longing to fulfil other creative impulses; it could deepen her sexuality, because there are many things about childbearing and childrearing that are deeply sensual; it could deepen her longing for a different kind of love.

I was beginning to get the sense that I was grappling with things not permitted, with taboos. Aren't there some women for whom nurturing is largely a series of exhausting mechanical acts with only the occasional sublime moment dashing past, when she's too worn out to notice? And aren't such mothers just as real as the hockey-stick kind? In fact, do the hockey-stick mothers even exist?

The feminist theorist Julia Kristeva suggests that our idea of motherhood is shrouded in a nostalgic fantasy of childhood, a territory that, now we're adults, is irretrievably lost. Because of this nostalgia, 'The mother is a nameless receptacle, an enveloping ground of identity which has no identity of its own. The mother remains locked within a speechless body.'[2]

Is the mother actually speechless? Or has our culture insisted she is? Or that, if she speaks, she speaks only in the way we long for, or dread?

As a reader there's a moment of joy when a writer says something so searingly true that everything jolts to a halt. I, as a reader, want to blurt out: 'So it's all right to say that!' I wanted that with mother stories.

When I held myself up to the light and discovered the gap where what I'm calling the 'real' mother stories ought to be, I did what comes naturally to many women – I began to doubt myself. I must've been reading the wrong things, I thought. People more up-to-date and literate than me, people who don't have to spend hours a day playing hide and seek and join-the-dots, would know about these stories. So I asked around: Where are the stories about mothers? People said of course there were many, and directed me to what seemed to be only the lost territory of the adult. So I said: But where are the stories about what it's really like for a woman to be with a young child? My friends without children looked puzzled and said: You mean stories about women washing dirty nappies?

It's a linguistic commonplace that the language we use constructs and defines our picture of the universe. If the whole state of motherhood is a nostalgic blur, I reasoned, I had to find my own language to focus the blur. At last I managed to say that I was looking for stories about the drama of the bond.

In all the stories I'd read, the bond between mother and child was assumed; it was a given, fixed state. The good mother loved her child. If her bond with the child was tested, it was only because of logistical difficulties – the woman was oppressed, she lived in nightmarish circumstances, there were too many nappies to wash. I couldn't find a sense of an evolving bond, one that can seem as ephemeral as the above-ground life of the cicada, as invisible as a star in another galaxy is to the naked eye. A bond that sometimes doesn't exist at all. There was no sense of a process. No sense of a drama, with all the escalation of a drama – the terror, the hubris, the recurring patterns, the comedy, the painful hilarity, sometimes the tragedy, often fraught and fragile compromises. No sense of a desperate love affair, with all the tensions of a love affair; one that may be just as emotionally intimate as the love between adults, and certainly more incessant, more invasive. I wanted a story examining the drama for a mother when she begins to allow a young child into her life, more importantly into the precious space of her mind, not on her terms, but on the child's terms, in its time, in its way.

The bond between mother and child may structure everything in human relations for the developing child. But what about the mother? I can't believe she's just a passive onlooker. She's been through the same experience herself and has been marked by it, created by it, perhaps scarred by it. If we are to believe Freud and Lacan, she is, in fact, the product of her bond with her mother. So who is she while her child is in her arms and what does she feel about the process? How does it fit into her life, her psyche, her memories, her desires for other things...isn't this momentous stuff? Yet we don't tell stories about it. It's as if we're all pretending there's no story here, while every woman who has ever been a mother must be criss-crossed by a vast network of experiences full of unexplored metaphors about their bonds with their children, experiences that could be the subject of art.

At your very first conversation with a keeper of the canon of great literature, you realise that however far women may have come in other ways, the bond between mothers and babies is simply not seen as a fit subject for a worthy novel. That nineteenth-century idea about art and the 'fit subject' is still with us; the artist must be isolationist, anti-domestic, full of the sublime forces of untamed nature.

These days a woman is sometimes allowed to be that. But not a mother. Not a mother writer, who flouts her state. This silence is harmful not only to women artists who might otherwise make rich and powerful metaphors of their experience, or to mothers who hold themselves up to the light and find no relevant stories that help them know who they are. It is a mutilation of writing itself.

Before I'd read Patti Miller's image, I was ready to send my downstairs book, the baby diary, off. We were all envisaging it in the baby-care section of the bookshops. Another resource book, not a story. I rang my agent to say that the book wasn't on its way, I put the postbag back in the cupboard, I took the bulldog clips out and found the scissors. I was whimpering with rage, but also with a wild exhilaration, because I was heading into exotic territory. Mothers. I could see that stories of mothers and babies are almost unsayable, unwritable, that we can barely speak for ourselves, because we are talking out of a long silence.

I began, in a certain terror, to cut up my diary, not knowing where this might lead, but knowing that I had to write a story about the drama of the bond. I knew I couldn't speak for other women, I could only speak for myself. But there might be many of us. Other women might be focusing the blur too, and be writing these secret stories, and soon, we might all be criss-crossed with stories about whatever real mothering is.

All the time I'd been considering these matters, the novel I'd been writing about the woman mathematician was waiting. She'd been silent and patient in my upstairs room for months, almost as if she didn't exist. And now, unexpectedly, so stealthily that I didn't even see the dust as she shook herself free, so silently that the floorboards were still, my mathematician heroine from upstairs crept down the stairs and entered the diary I'd just cut up.

In 1997, Sue Woolfe published Leaning Towards Infinity, *a novel about mothering, mathematics, and the drama of the bond.*

1   Elizabeth Grosz in *Jacques Lacan: A Feminist Introduction*, Allen and Unwin, 1990.
2   Quoted by Elizabeth Grosz in *Jacques Lacan*, op cit.

Claudette Johnson
How Many Do You Have Now?

As the sole black artist in my year and one of only three in the entire Fine Arts department, I became aware that black culture was considered alien, and could therefore be ignored, or exotic and subsequently misconstrued. The 'otherness' constructed for me by this process meant that significant issues about race and representation in my work were never satisfactorily addressed. A conference of black art students, held at the polytechnic during my final year, showed that my experience was shared by many other black art students. If a 'norm' existed for art students, then I, and many other black art students, stood outside of it.

Throughout my childhood I had absorbed the myth that great art was produced by great white men, a myth that has created the conditions for the invisibility of black women artists. I also gained the sense that artists who conceived or attempted to conceive, were in some way 'doomed'. According to George Boudaille, Paula Modersohn-Becker would have been accorded 'an important place in the history of the expressionist movement' but for her fatal attempt to have a child. While critical assessment of Berthe Morisot's work is a footnote to the description of the birth of her children and her activities as 'hostess' during the visits of ... 'Renoir, Monet,

Whistler...and many other *famous* people' (my italics). The tragic view of their lives implicit in this kind of description encourages the belief that, like lemmings over the cliff, artists who choose to become mothers must sacrifice one identity for the other.

When I became a mother myself I gave very little thought to the effect that this would have on my perception of myself as an artist, or how other artists would perceive me. When I announced my first pregnancy one artist friend described me as 'brave'. It was 1985 and we were exhibiting at the ICA in an exhibition entitled 'The Thin Black Line'. The work of eleven women artists was crammed into a narrow corridor space graphically illustrating the tokenism that had brought us there. It was a process which, as Lubaina Himid has said, make us 'less invisible' rather than visible. The comment about my 'bravery' was in recognition of the energy necessary to maintain even this level of visibility.

Among contemporary black women artists I find myself in the minority as a mother. Perhaps in the face of a continuing battle against marginalisation and male historians baying for tragedy, many black women artists put off, or decide against having children. As a result I have found my experience of otherness intensified by having children. In the years immediately following the births of my two sons, male contemporaries simply stopped having any kind of meaningful dialogue with me. While some female contemporaries would ask 'How many do you have now?' This illustrates my experience of the lack of dialogue between artists who are mothers and those who are not. In the vacuum created by this absence, assumptions proliferate.

I do not feel that I have to sacrifice my life as an artist for my role as a mother. I have continued to draw, paint and exhibit, with the intricacies of my changing experience providing a valuable and sustaining resource. I feel there needs to be more debate around the issue of artists as mothers so that the still narrow definition of 'artist' could be enlarged. I would like to see the fog of myth, sentiment and fear that surrounds the state of motherhood cleared away to allow the reality of the artist/mother's experience to emerge.

Deborah Watson
Keeping It Real
Entries from the Artist's Diary

3.05 pm, Wednesday

It's grey outside and it's grey inside. I'm back from my cleaning job, which I do to support my child and my painting. I guess I could get a sugar daddy but I'm not very good at playing dumb.

Today, like every day for the last six weeks, there's been a battle raging inside me. I hate this feeling: the sickness, the tiredness, the 'I can't be bothered to do anything' feeling. I hate having sore breasts when I toss and turn at night; I hate the migraines and I hate the debate of 'Should I or shouldn't I?'

Every day I get more and more frustrated because I don't feel like painting, or making. 'But you're creating the most precious, amazing thing possible,' a voice keeps prodding me. To which I answer: 'No wonder I don't feel like painting then – most of my creative energy is taken up with making this baby!' But having babies don't pay the bills (someone should write a song about that). I want to paint, I want to make, I want to see the fruits of my labour now. Yes, Now! I'm very 'want, want, want,' but I'm also pregnant and my hormones are all over the place. Excuses, you may mutter, and I realise I'm a silly girl for getting myself into this fix, but I'm going to get out and not come here again. I don't like this space.

*

I know that being pregnant with my first child, who's now nine, was the impetus for my return to painting. Because I wanted him so much I persevered through the initial few sicky weeks and painted every day. It was wonderful. Of course I felt dreadful every morning but I still felt safe and protected. I lived with my aunt and she looked after me those first few months. Fathers, where are they, when you really need them...?

My painting progressed well and I even sold work to a shop in Oxford Street. I had to; I was a single mother on welfare and I had to be enterprising. But now, nearly ten years later – well, I've been there. No one prepared me for being a mother, let alone a single mother. The highs and the lows of motherhood, made me look anew at the world and experience it in a different way. Made me aware that while some people respect the Mother and Child, others don't give a damn.

I paint embryos, Madonnas, icons to empower myself and others like me; attempting to balance the scales in an unjust society. But inside I feel like crying because I'm afraid. It's just so damn hard bringing up a child on your own. And still wanting to paint, and do other things too.

I hate these first few months of pregnancy and I'm not sure if I want to go on making babies on my own any more. Of course, it takes two to fertilise, but once that egg has embedded itself that's it. The man can do a runner if he's that way inclined.

So what will I do? I resent not having the energy to make the pictures that are in my head but I don't know what to do about it.

Or, rather, I do.

*

11.00 p.m. Tuesday
A couple of weeks have passed now and I've done it, had the abortion (though I don't want to write about that now). No, I'm no longer pregnant – but I am still a mother. Still a mother, still an artist, still a painter. Still trying to juggle my energy and my time. I wonder if Picasso or Gauguin ever had to help someone with their homework while cooking the dinner or doing the washing...Maybe I'd get to be called a prolific painter, a great painter, if I had women cooking my dinner or cleaning the floor or taking the children to school. I snatch pockets of time to paint and while I teach I share techniques, working on my own pieces and getting others involved.

Being a mother has made me look more closely at gender and gender politics in an 'on the bus' kind of way. (In an 'on the bus with a baby on my hip and will someone please stand up and give me seat!' way.) And so I paint mothers, babies, women, babies because I want to see more images of mothers and pregnant women. I need to paint more chubby women, and painfully thin ones, a more diverse range of mother-hood: Mary, Madonna, the Goddess. The source of creativity. Deep like the ocean She is. *La Mer*, Mary, the Sea...

Beeban Kidron
What About ME?

The body in my bed is not my own. Curled around me is Noah whose journey through beaded curtains and uncarpeted stairs to find mother warmth was heralded by the baby monitor. My dreams were not my own. Blaze called out – first for her daddy and then for an orange. Her daddy is not here, he lives elsewhere, and in my house even the insistent cry of a two-year-old does not produce an orange before 7.30am. My journeys through cold corridors and up unwelcoming treads to cover a child whose blankets have been kicked off, or to accompany a restless bladder to the toilet, render me blank as the canvas on which I intended to make my mark.

My children know not to shout before mummy has warmed herself into something human with her coffee. Three breakfasts, three bodies to dress, three sets of plans for the day. Fifteen minutes of numbers and letters; my paper, delivered, remains unread. The illuminated clock on the wall inches slowly to a time when I can expect reinforcements. I hand over Blaze and try to get Noah to school before the Lollipop man crosses to the other side of the zebra crossing – a sure sign that we will get a late note – again.

The morning started three hours ago and my creative life has not yet begun.

LUNCHTIME

Slips by unnoticed. I struggle to finish a book, that somebody somewhere thinks would make a good film. It is inconsequential. Unnourishing. A waste of precious time, better spent trying to remember the stories that absorbed me on the carpeted landing of my family home. During my 'difficult teens' I read about worlds that were mysterious. Of fallen women and whores with hearts of gold. Then both birth and death seemed more tangible, whole communities had something to say about each character's destiny. It was not, as now, every woman for herself.

Perhaps I should read one of the pile of polished but illiterate scripts sitting in unopened, Fed-ex packages marked 'extremely urgent'. Or I could fantasize about having found the perfect project and try to work out how to mother my children in some far flung location whilst working 16–18 hours a day. Who will tuck them in, understand their language, our history, care about their growth?

The temptation to order a staircarpet is over-whelming. It would unite us during our restless nights. The texture should be comforting, no harsh man-made substances, it should be welcoming to the soft soles of little humans and their tired mothers. Thinking of feet reminds me that Noah needs an appointment with a foot surgeon. Four phone calls at least. How much time will it take? How many dehumanised automated answering services will it involve.

3.30pm

A time ingrained in the heart of every mother. School is out. Kate, my Kate, Noah's Kate, Blaze's Kate, the person who makes life possible, will pick up Noah. For me it is countdown time. Which of the many undone tasks should I tackle?

I remember the accolades, the admiration, the flowers when Noah was born. Five months of prep. Four months of filming. I was so pregnant I never made it back to my apartment. I was taken from JFK airport straight to hospital, my bags still circling unclaimed on the airport carousel.

Beth Israel is a particularly New York institution; geographically it serves some of Manhattan's poorest, yet it is also home to specialist doctors with innumerable qualifications and patients with inexhaustible health insurance. Even the thousands of dollars that the insurance company paid for me to have my baby could not get me a clean toilet or a dim light.

From my hospital bed I wrote pages of instructions to actors, the editor and the producer who were due to shoot 3-second unit shots in Times Square. My assistant arrived looking very young and frightened. She picked up my messages, left flowers, and fled. The father of my child(ren) begged me to stop making a film and just have a bloody baby – after 36 hours and an unspeakable amount of pain, I did. In the same 36 hours my obstetrician delivered 11 babies. The nurses changed shift five times. The midwife Sylvie never left my side. I was too exhausted to know how much my world had changed. By the time I got home my Hollywood colleagues had sent me so many flowers it looked as though someone had died. As I walked through the door the phone rang. It was a fellow film director, celebrated, successful and the father of five, 'What timing, what grace. *Maseltov*'.

TEATIME

As I walk in I shout 'Anybody I know here?' and the children excitedly call their names. Noah turns to Blaze and says with the authority of the first born 'I told you she was coming'. This is our routine; my place at the table is always laid whether I am eating or not, and the menu and the day discussed with equal solemnity. They like their food, my children. Unfortunately teatime in London is when people in Los Angeles arrive in their offices and pick up the phone.

The previous generation paved the way for my generation to gallop unheeded into jobs previously reserved for men. Being a woman was unhazardous; being a mother was quite a different matter. I am not always available. I no longer answer the phone on demand. The cute message from Noah on the machine makes enquirers doubt that I live at this number, and Blaze's penchant for answering the phone unaided to have rambling conversations makes even the most generous question their long-distance phone bill.

Men in Hollywood take photographs of their offspring out of their pockets faster than any Western hero ever drew a gun. Further questioning invariably reveals a wife who 'elected' to stay at home, or that they only see their children at the weekend. It's a tough business you know, you have to be at your desk, on the phone, at breakfast, lunch, dinner, screenings, on set . . . it's a tough business . . . for a mother.

BEDTIME

Is sometimes a victory – we survived another day. All tucked up, teeth brushed, books read, songs sung, experiences shared, world problems solved – 'why do houses fall down?', 'They don't darling', 'They do! I heard it on the radio news.' We discuss earthquakes, fault lines and foundations – I draw a breath.

Sometimes bedtime brings the terrible sadness of another day on which we failed to bake a cake, paint a mural, count to a hundred without making a mistake. Yet another day on which the big red bike failed to do a tour of duty. Sometimes bedtime is merely a break in my working day – followed by a return to the office. Sometimes it's the beginning of my adult life – a longed-for trip to the theatre, dinner with friends. Sometimes I am defeated by the distracting relentless day.

I have been up for 15 hours and the muse has yet to appear.

WEEKENDS

We can stay in our pyjamas all day. The trick is to undertake as little as possible. These are the days that pass in a bliss that is undoubtedly a nostalgic false memory of one's own childhood. These too are days that have to be shared with the children's father. After a week of wondering if anything will get done, I am listless with my freedom. Creativity, turns out to be a slave to routine and petulantly avoids the available gap, turning its back on me like an ignored lover. Sleep-deprived and fragile without the protective/demanding/distracting layer of my children, seduction is out of the question.

I enjoyed being pregnant. My body, proud for the second time, got enormous, no longer fat, ample or Rubenesque. Throwing up whilst location hunting or squatting behind the set to pee were small inconveniences. The life force in me gave me an acute ear, a brimming empathy for my characters and those that played them. I ran up mountains and waded off the Cornish coast at midnight in waters so cold that I began to feel my child would be able to withstand anything.

Only two things got in the way of this consuming creativity. My guilt at abandoning Noah aged 18 months, to the care of others; at being a mother so tired that on the few occasions I was able to race from set in time to read his bedtime book I would fall asleep in mid-sentence again and again despite his repeated prodding. The other was the studio executive's obsession with my cascading hormones. Every objection, request or disagreement was the fault of 'the hysterical woman with child'. I can think of no word in the English language that describes the sensation of knowing in advance that you will be misunderstood, not because of the content of one's speech nor its tone – but simply because I was pregnant.

HOLIDAYS

Unbelievably they come around again. No sooner have you perfected your term-time childcare and stolen every possible moment for your working life, then along comes another holiday.

I can't help wondering about times past – in all the marching and agitating to create opportunities in the public world for women, who did we think was going to bring up the children? We expect and are expected to work. We travel further, do longer hours. Live in streets where our neighbors are strangers. We are a generation of individuals. Our lives are not structured (for the most part) by civic, religious or familial duty. Where are we to find the energy for our children, our collective future? I was fortunate enough to end up with work that I love. Was it greedy to have children, a stake in the future, genetic continuity, unconditional love given and received? The humour and irreverent curiosity that they bring? As I build my fifth sandcastle, I look at the man asleep under his paper while his wife gets buried in the sand. I wonder if the pleasure of children is something only creative men can afford.

I have been overwhelmed in Italy, France, the US, South America, the Middle East, my own home at Christmas, Easter, August, Spring/Summer/Autumn half term. Overwhelmed by the need to entertain, the mountain of luggage, chicken pox, spider bites, the heat, the cold, their desire to shit with no toilet in sight and no power to control themselves. I have been overwhelmed by having to carry sleeping children too far, staying for a week at the edge of a precipice which called my toddler to it. Overwhelmed by the annoyance of strangers who have travelled to escape the shrill sounds of children playing; by buses that won't stop, cafés that won't serve, hotels that won't house, children.

I want to feel heat on my skin, taste new foods, see first hand the colours of my imagination. At night in India, 17 years old and alone, I would feel the burden of my youth and gender and would stay firmly inside, safe with the cockroaches, my candle and my diary. As I grew older I travelled with men and the night became available to me. Men on the street looked with curiosity or envy at another man's prize. Now again I am confined to quarters in strange lands – by sleeping children. Confined to short adventures, the shady side of the street, places with a restaurant nearby. Travel is no longer the periodic wanderings of an inquisitive mind. We have holidays to 'destinations', at peak times and peak prices. But...just as I despair...Noah points out the desert sand is made up of a multitude of different colours whilst the blue of the sea merges perfectly with the blue of the sky. I turn around to see Blaze lying on the ground, indenting the earth with her small presence. 'That's Blazey' she points out as she stands to survey the indistinct shape. It is all the sensory help I need. Children have an eye for detail. That indentation is me too.

WORK

Is more difficult, fractured, elusive. The muse used to be easier to capture. My reserves of energy were legendary. My name and presence individual. Now I am often referred to as somebody's mummy. I am joined to so many others and separated from myself. But now I have seen language emerge twice, I give clear instructions to the writers with whom I collaborate. The famous and ' famously difficult' are never further from my grasp than a two year old with an unreasonable desire and the unfathomable emotional excess with which to pursue it. Perspective, literalism, surrealism, unfettered imagination, the incredible creative abandon of a child's mind are all there to borrow and steal from.

To bring joy and understanding was my original task. Now, not only in my work, but also in every detail of my life, I have an audience, neither faceless nor nameless – there is creativity in every corner and crevice. But what about ME – the person who existed before childbirth and gravity had their way?

NIGHT

My body twitches with exhaustion. My mind is tripping. I have stayed up beyond 3 a.m. reading something beautiful and purposeful. It would make a wonderful film. Set in another time and another place, it makes more sense of now than any of the newsprint that I read. I am alight with possibility as I check the doors and windows, the baby gate and the nightlights. Am I gamekeeper or ghost? My children lie in abandoned sleep, they couldn't be more beautiful. I bend down to kiss each of them as I rearrange limbs and blankets. As I imagine the encroaching morning I fall prey to the ludicrous hope that the children will sleep late. I laugh (quietly of course). They will wake early, I will need coffee, another day will begin. In my secular fashion I pray. Pray that they too will grow to find satisfaction and inspiration in a day like today.

Käthe Kollwitz
from **The Diary and Letters of Käthe Kollwitz**

September 1, 1911

I imagine the following sculpture as utterly beautiful: a pregnant woman chiseled out of stone. Carved only down to the knees so that she looks the way Lise said she did the time she was pregnant with Maria: 'As if I am rooted to the ground.' The immobility, restraint, introspection. The arms and hands dangling heavily, the head lowered, all attention directed inward. And the whole thing in heavy, heavy stone. Title: *Pregnancy*.

New Year's Day, 1912

... What about myself? Summing up of 1911? Progress? No progress in my relationship with Karl. What he always speaks of, what seems to him still the sole worthwhile goal of our long living together – that we should grow together in the deepest intimacy – I still do not feel and probably never will learn to feel.

Are not the ties with the boys also growing slacker? I almost think so. For the last third of life there remains only work. It alone is always stimulating, rejuvenating, exciting and satisfying. This year I have made excellent progress in sculpture. I can see an advance between the first group of Mother with Child and the last finished group. This group, in which the child sits between the mother's legs and she holds his feet with her left hand, is about done as far as working from the model goes. Now I have taken it up again; but it still has a dead side that I do not know how to attack.

August 27, 1914
In the heroic stiffness of these times of war, when our feelings are screwed to an unnatural pitch, it is like a touch of heavenly music, like sweet, lamenting murmurs of peace, to read that French soldiers spare and actually help wounded Germans, that in the *franc-tireur* villages German soldiers write on the walls of houses such notices as: Be considerate! An old woman lives here. These people were kind to me. Old people only. Woman in child-bed. And so on.

A piece by Gabriele Reuter in the *Tag* on the tasks of women today. She spoke of the joy of sacrificing – a phrase that struck me hard. Where do all the women who have watched so carefully over the lives of their beloved ones get the heroism to send them to face the cannon? I am afraid that this soaring of the spirit will be followed by the blackest despair and dejection. The task is to bear it not only during these few weeks, but for a long time – in dreary November as well, and also when spring comes again, in March, the month of young men who wanted to live and are dead. That will be much harder.

Those who now have only small children, like Lise her Maria, seem to me so fortunate. For us, whose sons are going, the vital thread is snapped

September 30, 1914
Cold, cloudy autumnal weather. The grave mood that comes over one when one knows: there is war, and

one cannot hold on to any illusions any more. Nothing is real but the frightfulness of this state, which we almost grow used to. In such times it seems so stupid that the boys must go to war. The whole thing is so ghastly and insane. Occasionally there comes the foolish thought: how can they possibly take part in such madness? And at once the cold shower: they *must, must!* All is levelled by death; down with all the youth! Then one is ready to despair.

Only one state of mind makes it at all bearable: to receive the sacrifice into one's will. But how can one maintain such a state?

[Peter Kollwitz was killed on October 22, 1914.]

December 1, 1914
Conceived the plan for a memorial for Peter tonight, but abandoned it again because it seemed to me impossible of execution. In the morning I suddenly thought of having Reike ask the city to give me a place for the memorial. There would have to be a collection taken for it. It must stand on the heights of Schildhorn, looking out over the Havel. To be finished and dedicated on a glorious summer day. Schoolchildren of the community singing, 'On the way to pray'. The monument would have Peter's form, lying stretched out, the father at the head, the mother at the feet. It would be to commemorate the sacrifice of all the young volunteers.

It is a wonderful goal, and no one has more right than I to make this memorial.

December 9, 1914
My boy! On your memorial I want to have your figure on top, *above* the parents. You will lie outstretched,

holding out your hands in answer to the call for sacrifice: 'Here I am.' Your eyes – perhaps – open wide, so that you see the blue sky above you, and the clouds and birds. Your mouth smiling. And at your breast the pink I gave you.

November 1915

I am reading Walter Heymann – his poems and letters from the front. Again I feel quite distinctly that it is not proper for me to lament over the war. Certainly I know what it is *like*. But I may not complain. No one may for whom the dearest person in the world has gone, as Peter went. Heymann's wife surely does not complain. Nor would it be right for her to. It is right for us to weep for our loved ones, but we must be worthy heirs. We may also be against the war. We may work – must help work – so that this one will be the last. But I must stop giving way to this type of personal grief.

December 1915

The idea of eternity and immortality doesn't mean anything to me at present. The spirit in Peter goes on living. True enough – but what does this spirit mean to him? The great world spirit which entered into him and which goes on working after its dwelling is shattered – that is something not conceivable. What was important was this particular form which grew. This unique person, this human being who could live only once. What continues is spirit in itself, but yet not Peter's spirit. Peter's spirit was inseparable from his body. That is why for me there is no consolation at all in the thought of immortality. The one consolation would be to believe in a personal continuance of life. Then one would have to imagine that the great spirit embodied itself in a similar form, so that one caught the breath of something again when one came across such a person. – If he had had a child, there would be traces of him left.

When one says so simply that someone has 'lost his life' – what a meaning there is in that – to lose one's life.

January 2, 1916
Recently Karl said, 'His death has made us no better.' The narrowness in me – that is the worst. To extend, expand, become something higher – that is what one asks of oneself. To remain the same person one was before fate struck – this must not be. Transformation through a single act of will has not come about. Therefore it must take place slowly.

January 17, 1916
...Where are my children now? What is left to their mother? One boy to the right and one to the left, my right son and my left son, as they called themselves. One dead and one so far away, and I cannot help him, cannot give to him out of myself. All has changed forever. Changed, and I am impoverished. My whole life as a mother is really behind me now. I often have a terrible longing to have it back again – to have children, my boys, one to the right and one to the left; to dance with them as formerly when spring arrived and Peter came with flowers and we danced a springtide dance.

April 18, 1916
Last night I dreamed once more that I had a baby. There was much in the dream that was painful, but

I recall one sensation distinctly. I was holding the tiny infant in my arms and I had a feeling of great bliss as I thought that I could go on always holding it in my arms. It would be one year old and then only two, and I would not have to give it away.

April 19, 1916
Worked. I am making progress on the mother. I think about little Peter's consoling words to me: 'Don't worry, Mother, it will be beautiful too.'

Good Friday, April 20, 1916
In Peter's room. Then I drove out to Heinersdorf and from there walked a while in the direction of Malchow. A country road lined with willows. Up in the branches of one of them five boys crouched. To the left, broad, open fields. Peter certainly walked along this road. I heard larks singing. There was such a feeling of tranquillity in me that I thought: if age brings with it this peace, then I understand why old people do not voluntarily depart from life. Younger, still active people see in the old only strength decaying, but the old person himself experiences something new in himself, the peace of God which more and more fills him. If that is so, stagnation is only an outward illusion; the old person himself has the valid feeling of further development, and this keeps him from putting an end to his life. It always comes back to this: that only one's inner feelings represent the truth. The feelings of age, not yet being experienced, are still a foreign realm to us. It is an 'impertinence toward life' in Keller's sense to see no value in age.

August 22, 1916
Stagnation in my work.

When I feel so parched, I almost long for the sorrow again. And then when it comes back I feel it stripping me physically of all the strength I need for work.

Made a drawing: the mother letting her dead son slide into her arms. I might make a hundred such drawings and yet I do not get any closer to him. I am seeking him. As if I had to find him in the work. And yet everything I can do is so childishly feeble and inadequate. I feel obscurely that I could throw off this inadequacy, that Peter is somewhere in the work and I might find him. And at the same time I have the feeling that I can no longer do it. I am too shattered, weakened, drained by tears. I am like the writer in Thomas Mann: he can only write, but he has not sufficient strength to live what is written. It is the other way round with me. I no longer have the strength to form what has been lived. A genius and a Mann could do it. I probably cannot.

For work, one must be hard and thrust outside oneself what one has lived through. As soon as I begin to do that, I again feel myself a mother who will not give up her sorrow. Sometimes it all becomes so terribly difficult.

August 27, 1916
Read an essay on liberalism by Leopold von Wiese. It showed me all the contradictory elements within myself. My untenably contradictory position on the war. How did I come to it? Because Peter sacrificed his life. What I saw so clearly then and what I wanted to preserve in my work now seems to be once more so dubious. I think I can keep Peter only if I do not let

anyone take away from me what he taught me then. Now the war has been going on for two years and five million young men are dead, and more than that number again are miserable, their lives wrecked. Is there *anything at all* that can justify that?

And now Wiese speaks of the necessity of 'opposing utterly all sacrifice of the living to a lifeless idea'. 'For a pair of happy eyes means more than all the doctrines of worldly wisdom.' Surely that is something different from the joy in the law with which Peter and his fellows marched into the field. And different from what Rupp taught: 'Man is not born for happiness, but to do his duty.'

October 11, 1916
Everything remains as obscure as ever for me. Why is that? It's not only our youth who go willingly and joyfully into the war; it's the same in all nations. People who would be friends under other conditions now hurl themselves at one another as enemies. Are the young really without judgement? Do they always rush into it as soon as they are called? Without looking closer? Do they rush into war because they want to, because it is in their blood so that they accept without examination whatever reasons for fighting are given to them? Do the young want war? Would they be old before their time if they no longer wanted it?

This frightful insanity – the youth of Europe hurling themselves at one another.

When I think I am convinced of the insanity of the war, I ask myself again by what law man ought to live. Certainly not in order to attain the greatest possible happiness. It will always be true that life must be subordinated to the service of an ideal. But in this case, where has that principle led us? Peter, Erich, Richard, all have subordinated their lives to the idea of patriotism. The English, Russian and French young men have done the same. The consequence has been this terrible killing, and the impoverishment of Europe. Then shall we say that the youth in all these countries have been cheated? Has their capacity for sacrifice been exploited in order to bring on the war? Where are the guilty? Are there any? Or is everyone cheated? Has it been a case of mass madness? And when and how will the awakening take place?

I shall never fully understand it all. But it is clear that our boys, our Peter, went into the war two years ago with pure hearts, and that they were ready to die for Germany. They died – almost all of them. Died in Germany and among Germany's enemies – by the millions.

February 4, 1917
I've worked. On the father. Before I left I removed the cloths covering Peter's head. The head is turned to one side. The blanket still lay over the body. Emerging out of the wholly wrapped-up figure, his head looked utterly beautiful, with his serious, devout smile. Perhaps I shall do the work so that the entire body is wrapped in a blanket and only the head left free.

February 9, 1917
Today circumstances forced me to interrupt the work on the father and take up the plaster cast of the mother. Sawed off the head and placed it experimentally in an entirely different position. Possibly what I said will come about – that by continuing to work on the plaster I shall be able to

raise myself above the average in one spot first and then, sticking to that, gradually pull up the other parts of the work. Climbing like a snail, creeping, taking the tiniest steps, but at least going *upward*.

February 1917

Yesterday I attended an evening of readings by Durieux and Eysold at Cassirer's. Everything was pretty dull, except that Durieux read a story by Leonhard Frank about a waiter who had an only son. The son falls 'on the field of honour'. And then afterwards, at a social democratic meeting, the waiter suddenly finds words. The procession on the streets, growing; 'they want to make peace.' The enormous stir of the people at the end, and the sounding bells, 'Peace, peace, peace!' It was unendurable. When she stopped reading, a man's voice cried out again and again, 'Peace, peace, peace!'

To know all this, to know that the longing for peace is so fervent everywhere in Europe, the same everywhere, and yet the war *cannot* stop and goes on day after day, and every hour young men must die!

July 1917

When I told Karl that Wertheimer may visit Peter's grave, Karl said he would like Peter to have a gravestone. I said, then I should like to make it. Today I thought about it again. I thought that the relief of the parents might be set upon his grave. Then I realised that this relief would be more appropriate for the whole cemetery. It belongs up front at the entrance. A square stone, the relief cut into the face. Life size. Below or above it: Here lies German youth. Or: Here lie Germany's finest young men. Or: Here lie the youthful dead. Or simply: Here lie the young.

It seems to me *I must carry this out*. God grant I keep my health until it is all done for Peter and the others.

July 26, 1917
Work is still going very well. I work without effort and without tiring. It is as if a fog had lifted. Now for the first time I am beginning to understand plaster work. I know what it is all about and what one can aim at. If nothing unusual interferes, I think I shall really be finished with the woman this fall. Sufficiently so for the stone work to be done after the plaster. And once I really have one figure finished, once I have really solved one, I will be able to make the others. Possibly then I can finish the work next year.

I have seen now that plaster work is not only filing away at the plaster cast which has been made from the clay, but an independent task in its own right. This time I will not attempt to perfect my clay model of the man, but as soon as the general outlines are fixed I shall have it cast in plaster and then finish it. How long it has taken me to realise this.

June 25, 1919
Today prepared everything for the abandonment of my big work. Tomorrow it will all be taken down. With what firm faith I set to work, and now I am stopping. As I stood up on the scaffold beside Peter and saw his sweet, smiling face, his air of devotion, and then thought of all the time I had worked, of all the love and aspiration, all the many tears that are frozen into that work, I promised him again: I will come back, I shall do this work for you, for you and

the others. It is only postponed. But this promise no longer has the old intensity. I do not know whether I will live long enough and keep strong enough to finish the work. The fact that now is no time for such a memorial does not matter to me. The years pass, and what was then sacred remains. If people cannot see this now, they will see it again later on.

As I kissed Peter's face and bade goodbye to the work, I thought of Germany. For Germany's cause was his cause, and Germany's cause is lost now as my work is lost. No, not really lost. If I am permitted to live and see Peter's work done and done well, commemorating him and his friends in some beautiful place – then perhaps that will signify that Germany too has passed out of the most difficult time.

January 4, 1920
I have again agreed to make a poster for a large-scale aid programme for Vienna. I hope I can make it, but I do not know whether I can carry it out because it has to be done quickly and I feel an attack of grippe coming on.

I want to show Death. Death swings the lash of famine – people, men, women and children, bowed low, screaming and groaning, file past him.

While I drew, and wept along with the terrified children I was drawing, I really felt the burden I am bearing. I felt that I have no right to withdraw from the responsibility of being an advocate. It is my duty to voice the sufferings of men, the never-ending sufferings heaped mountain-high. This is my task, but it is not an easy one to fulfil. Work is supposed to relieve you. But is it any relief when in spite of my poster people in Vienna die of hunger every day? And when I know that? Did I feel relieved when I made the prints on war and knew that the war would go on raging? Certainly not. Tranquillity and relief have come to me only when I was engaged on one thing: the big memorial for Peter. Then I had peace and was with him.

April 22, 1931
Today was the opening of the Academy show in which I am exhibiting the two sculptures – the father and mother.

This is a great divide, a highly significant period. For years I worked on them in utter silence, showed them to no one, scarcely even to Karl and Hans; and now I am opening the doors wide so that as many people as possible may see them. A big step which troubles and excites me; but it has also made me very happy because of the unanimous acclaim of my fellow artists. I am thinking mainly of the sculptures. These past weeks have been very strenuous. But now that the works are delivered to the world, I am calmer. In June I will start on the finishing touches. In the fall – Peter – I shall bring it to you.

April 16, 1932
A good day. Richter, the state architect, came to the studio in response to a letter I had written to the cemetery board in Brussels. He looked at the work and thought it very good. He told me that the construction of the pedestal and the laying of the foundation will be undertaken by the cemetery board. He will also take care of getting the works put through custom-free and of the freight charges in Belgium. The German national railway will probably provide free transportation.

July 23, 1932. In Belgium.
Saturday we drove to the cemetery (Herr Schult, young Lingner, Karl and I). The first impression of the cemetery was strange, because it has been changed since I last saw it. It has been levelled. And it seems smaller because the unknown soldiers have all been buried in pairs. Now it has been turned into a regular rectangle. The small tin crosses have been replaced by somewhat larger wooden crosses. The rows run with perfect regularity, but the space between the crosses is not always equal. A small stone bridge leads across the highway. The stone wall is higher on the highway side. Inside, it is lower, convenient for sitting. The wall is made of laid stones between which varieties of moss are growing. Now the cemetery seems more monotonous than it did. Only three crosses are planted with roses. On Peter's grave they are in bloom, red ones. It is nice that the whole area is now planted to grass. The space in front, which has been reserved for the figures, is smaller than I thought. It too is in lawn.

In the right corner of the cemetery the granite stones are still lying packed up. The workers from the graves' committee were there. The stone pedestals, already cut, were lying in readiness, and the provisional wooden pedestals. The dummies were being set up. First the woman, then the man. Long discussions on how much space to leave between; finally everything was settled. So that the whole will combine and the parents will have crosses in front and all around them like a flock, Lingner persuaded me that six more graves should be brought up, so that there would be no gap between the figures and the crosses. There are still many remains not yet put in rows...

The British and Belgian cemeteries seem brighter, in a certain sense more cheerful and cosy, more familiar than the German cemeteries. I prefer the German ones. The war was not a pleasant affair; it isn't seemly to prettify with flowers the mass deaths of all these young men. A war cemetery ought to be sombre.

The day before, Schult visited the cemeteries in Northern France. At Arras there is one that holds 30,000 graves. It has one large mass grave which contains 2000 soldiers. Schult's companion said that you can scarcely see the limits of the cemetery; you have the impression that it goes on to infinity.

The following day the figures were set up. The workers were already waiting, the blocks were in place. It took long, hard work before the figure of the woman was raised. It turned out that the figure had to be raised somewhat to get the proper forward view, because the gently rising terrain emphasised the lean of the figure. Then the man. The great trouble with him, which at first upset me terribly, was that his line of vision is not high enough. He is not looking out over the whole cemetery; instead he is staring down, brooding. The hours of work were very tiring. When we left I was sad rather than happy.

Friday morning it rained and I packed. In the afternoon it cleared. Van Hauten came with the car around four o'clock and we drove out there once more – for the last time. And the depression of the day before lifted. I was able to see it all in the right light. We said goodbye.

Kate Paul
Motherhood as Creativity

After working as an actress for twelve years, I gave up my career when I became a mother. It is a decision I often find myself justifying. Deciding not to work is a strong statement in any circumstances; and deciding to look after one's child in preference to working provokes strong reactions. Working mothers sometimes ask me how I can stand it. At its most extreme, there is a feeling that by not working I am failing to exercise my rights, and so betraying what women have been working towards for the last century.

Historically, women were seen as supporters and carers rather than doers. This passive role is epitomised by Chaucer's Patient Griselda: the ideal woman, she suffers any amount of abuse and hardship in order to continue serving her family. And there are still connotations of a rather unhealthy selflessness in motherhood: as if, by concentrating on one's children, one is ignoring one's own needs, like Philip Larkin's young mothers in 'Afternoons', pushed to the sides of their own lives. Indeed, other mothers have often told me that I should 'do something for myself'. In the past, all I wanted to do was act. I used to be miserable when not working; and now I am constantly amazed at this huge change in myself.

I never anticipated giving up acting. Before my daughter was born I had every intention of working again at the earliest opportunity because I simply could not imagine *not* being an actress: that was who I was, how I defined myself. I certainly believed I would feel trapped, resenting both my child and my partner, if I was forced to stay at home doing jigsaw puzzles. And there's no doubt I do feel resentful at times – it's absolutely not the case that I have discovered myself to be some dream mother, always serene, cheerful and understanding. On the contrary, I've discovered in myself depths of ill-humour and impatience I never knew I possessed. Nevertheless, after four years, I was still resisting the idea of working again, clinging instead to my days alone with my daughter. (Well, hardly alone; the social life of a pre-schooler is frantic.)

During Molly's babyhood I put this lack of motivation down to breast-feeding and hormones. Now I am forced to reassess the situation. It is not that I don't miss activity – I do. But I have come to realise that what I'm doing now is not merely a worthwhile alternative – it actually satisfies the same craving to be creative that acting did. This satisfaction does not stem from the countless ways in which mothers are forced to be creative: the endless leaf-printing, finger-painting, cookie baking and model making, not to mention more improvisation and imaginative role-playing in one week than would be considered necessary in three years at drama school. The satisfaction comes from living and breathing the creative process of the developing relationship with my child, and the part that plays in preparing her for other relationships. No other stimulation is necessary; the satisfaction and joy of being a mother is probably the most creative part of my life, and I feel very fortunate to be able to devote my time to it.

This feeling is extraordinarily strong during pregnancy and immediately after the baby is born. The sense of achievement is like nothing in the world: 'We made that!' It can be more difficult to sustain that joy during the first couple of years. I think back to all the days of exhaustion and depression associated with looking after a baby or young child; days when you feel you've achieved a huge amount if you manage to get the washing done. It's not easy to feel part of a creative process at times like that. Nevertheless, as the baby grows, so does the sense of satisfaction that accompanies the shaping of a personality, the ability to influence what someone will be in the world, and the knowledge that their achievements will develop partly from one's own input. It is a joy to watch the principles of, for example, kindness and respect, which one attempts to instil in a child, starting to take root and grow, no longer a repetition, half comprehended, but spontaneous and fully realised. And, after all, any piece of work goes through its difficult stages; it doesn't make the end result any less rewarding.

This is beginning to sound a little like a Frankenstein complex – the idea of creating a living being according to one's own specifications. The reality is totally different, of course. You cannot make your child into the person you want her to be any more than you can live her life for her. The process is a creative collaboration.

The common image of a creative person is the writer or painter in a lonely garret, struggling in isolation. But, in theatre at least, the main joy of the creative process is through collaboration. This was something I found quite hard when I started acting. Not content with learning my own lines and doing the best job I could, I felt I had a responsibility for the entire production. If someone was late in learning their part I was in agonies of apprehension; if another actor interpreted his role in a way that I disagreed with, I felt a duty to thrash the matter out in endless arguments. I wanted the show to be perfect and it was down to me to make that possible. I only started thoroughly enjoying my work when I learned to accept that I was part of a whole creative team working together and could only influence the final quality of the production by making my own performance as good as I was able. From then on, the excitement of working with my fellow cast members became the most stimulating part of the work.

I have had a strangely similar experience in my four years as a mother. It is a collaborative process and there is only so much you can do. I have to stand back and watch my daughter live through her problems and even her fears. I can offer words of comfort, and physical protection, but it will be experience rather than words that will eventually teach her that there is no need to be afraid of cats, pigeons, babies, or the noisy drier in the ladies' loo. The fulfilment comes from being part of the team working towards the final production. Not the director; just a member of the cast.

In fact, I have very recently started working again. Not acting, but some writing. I have chosen a line of work that involves me staying at home. Clearly, it's a sensible, practical choice, and means I can take my daughter to and from nursery. But, more than that, I also seem to feel a great sense of confidence working in the space where I have spent these years with my daughter and I feel that I have returned to work on my own terms, in a way that has not disrupted the pattern of our lives together, and at a time when both she and I are ready for it. I feel very privileged to be sitting at my desk, with my daughter beside me at her little red table, drawing endless pictures. I also feel immense satisfaction in working alongside her, as she is engaged in her own creative activity, independently developing her own skills and confidence as all children do. It is an arrangement which allows us both to thrive. On days when she goes out for the whole day with friends, I find I get no more work done than when she's at home with me, and at nursery for just a couple of hours. The frequent little interruptions – to make a snack, have a chat, admire her work or, of course, put on a video – seem to focus my mind. There is a real thrill at being able to get my work done, and yet continue the routine of our life together.

I have been comparing my sense of satisfaction and joy at being a mother with the feelings that acting gave me. But there is a difference – bringing up a child gives one no credit in the eyes of the world. It seems that creativity is assessed solely in terms of public output. The role of the mother is so utterly funda-mental, so deeply emotive and personal to everyone, that it is hard to be objective about one's feelings towards it: after all, the relationship with one's mother is the first, formative relationship of one's life. We tend to belittle motherhood almost as a way of bringing down to size our extraordinarily complex feelings about our own mothers and our own childhoods. But parenting is a positive choice; each child who is born brings something new and unique to the human race. As the mothers of these children we are releasing that new power and energy into the world.

Playing with my daughter may seem a very natural, even mundane, daily necessity. And yet playing, and having an input into a child's developing imagination, is much more than that. It contributes to the creative future of humanity. If we do not learn to be creative as children, we may never have another chance.

Laura Godfrey-Isaacs
The Advantages of Being a
Woman Artist

Motherhood and Art Don't Go! At least that is the idea
perpetuated by the art world and the media. The artist
is presented as a single-minded obsessive whose
dedication to making art cannot possibly be squared
with the demands of child rearing. Before I became a
mother I had always fought for equal rights and
representation, but as a mother things were fundamentally different. Not only had my day-to-day life
experience changed, but there was also a shift in my
sensibility and perspective, and issues that had once
seemed so clear to me became much more complicated.
Creativity certainly does not go away after the birth of a
child, but for me the notion of 'the artist' had to be
reconsidered and expanded, and this led to a personal
and political assessment of my role in cultural
production.

At first I thought that things would get back to
normal after the birth and planned accordingly. Like
most women I was completely unprepared for the
reality of motherhood. It is still amazing to me how
little women actually know about how tough it is.
There seems to be some form of denial which operates
before motherhood: as young women compete with
men they don't want to confront the real inequalities
which start once you have had a baby.

It was not until my wonderful, funny and much-loved daughter, Tallulah, was two years old that I realised the long-term reality of motherhood. The first two years were mostly concerned with survival. Extreme fatigue coupled with conflicting emotions of infatuation with my new baby and frustration at my lack of freedom conspired to keep me locked in crisis. I adored my baby but felt utterly alienated from the rest of my life and found it very hard to connect with my professional practice. However, I had more help than many new mothers: my family were very supportive and I was able to use a variety of childcare on a part-time basis. I was therefore able to work, albeit in a restricted way.

I felt dreadful most of the time during my pregnancy, and found it impossible to contemplate the physical demands of my usual studio practice. I took up knitting as a strategy to continue working in a medium that had long fascinated me and was not hindered by my changed physical situation. It was an activity I had always enjoyed as a child, creating enormous outsize jumpers which were really more to do with the process of making than the finished article. After Tallulah was born I could pick up my knitting while she was asleep or in the evenings; a classic and pragmatic way to use all those fragmented moments. I also got my mother and mother-in-law to knit for me, and later used ready-made knitted samples and secondhand knitwear from charity shops. In this way I was able to produce work at home and within the bounds of my restricted time.

Knitting has always been seen as a feminine, domestic and essentially amateur activity which comes very low in the craft hierarchy, let alone the high art hierarchy, and this lowly status interested me.

I also liked the irony of using knitting to make art at the very time when most women would be knitting something for their baby. My knitting produced non-functional objects which played with various formal devices in painting and sculpture. The end products were a very graphic representation of time, suggesting the amount of physical labour and investment bound up in the creation of the hand-crafted object.

Despite this, I still felt that I was very far away from my former self; the artist who would work in the studio for up to ten hours a day producing large series of works. I found myself producing single works which didn't always feel connected or coherent. Motherhood seemed to have impaired my ability to concentrate or plan long term (though this has lessened with time). I think I became so wrapped up in the demands of the present that I lost the ability to conceive of large projects in the future.

This loss of single-mindedness led to a lot of confusion in my work, and when Tallulah was two I started to have serious doubts about my future as an artist. How could I possibly compete with such limited time and a lack of concentration? I began to feel angry and depressed about the intractable conflict between motherhood and creativity. Many of the values and disciplines I had carried with me since art school now seemed ridiculous and irrelevant. The art world appeared to be full of those who promoted the empty, anti-political stance of the 'Young British Artist' whose lifestyle certainly didn't include children. I had lost confidence and perspective. I kept on thinking of the Guerrilla Girls piece, 'The Advantages of being a Woman Artist' – the advantages being: Working without the pressure of success, Having the opportunity to choose between career and motherhood, Not having to choke on those big cigars or paint in Italian suits...things seemed bleak.

One of the major difficulties for me was my own adherence to the idea of art as an overwhelmingly personal, cathartic and obsessional activity which demands time and attention to the exclusion of everything else. This could not be squared with the equally demanding presence of a child and my own desire to look after her. However, this model of the artist as a quasi-mythical figure who pursues art above all else was the one perpetuated throughout the art world. My desire to comply with this model was all the more ridiculous in that such a figure has always been presented as male – and this has changed little despite the increasing visibility of women artists. It is the same model that was promoted but never challenged when I was in art school in the 1980s.

At college I was the consummate 'good girl' producing endless figurative paintings which seemed to arise out of an insatiable desire to create work. The colleges I went to were incredibly uncritical places and were, at the time, dominated by middle-aged male tutors who did not seem to have the inclination to engage with radical forms of practice. There were certainly no discussions about gender or feminist art history. As a result I emerged from college unpoliticised and ignorant, modelling myself entirely on male artists. What radicalised my thinking was a year on a Fulbright Scholarship in New York, where I saw a range and ambition of work by female artists that had eluded me in London. There was work by women artists such as Cindy Sherman, for example, who plays with constructed femininity through photo series using her own body; or Barbara Kruger who uses the language of advertising to question the status and roles of women.

When I returned to England in 1990 I started to make paintings which mimicked the surface and visceral nature of the body. Piling on paint in hot pinks and red, the canvases became excessive surfaces suggesting contradictory responses to the female body – ranging from sensual enjoyment to disgust. I was interested to work within the tradition of oil painting because of its long-time association with the female body, the nude, predominantly presented by the male artist for the male gaze.

I reached the end of my investigations in paint fairly quickly and went on to explore a range of media and processes, from industrial materials such as polyurethane foam resin to children's materials such as plasticine and playdoh. These processes, which were highly labour intensive, obsessive, singular activities, were bound up with the myth of 'the original artist' and studio-based activity. And it was precisely this myth that was fundamentally challenged by motherhood.

But motherhood itself is surrounded by as many myths as the figure of the artist. The mother must be self-sacrificing, nurturing, morally correct and unsexual; the artist unconventional, self-obsessed, sexual and subversive. The artist is expected, indeed encouraged, to misbehave, living outside the normal structures of society, whereas the mother is presented as an essentially stabilising force. Even though all of these clichés have been challenged, their influence is still pervasive and a woman artist finds herself caught between the two roles. Many women artists before my generation chose not to have children or gave up their practice after giving birth (often to support their male partner's work). I think we are probably the first generation, with some notable exceptions, who have embraced the idea of being simultaneously a mother and an artist. We therefore have had to confront these outmoded models and seek new definitions.

After months of depression I made some vital shifts in my own thinking in order to unite the reality of my life and my desire to make art. Instead of fighting my circumstances and seeing them as a weakness, I tried to radicalise the relationship between the mother, the artist and the domestic sphere. After much consideration, I started to present exhibitions and events in my house, which I launched as a venue called 'home', and I shifted my role to encompass the presentation of art as well as its production. In this way, I am asserting the role of the home and domesticity at the heart of cultural production.

Since December 1998 I have run a series of collaborative projects with other artists and designers to present exhibitions, events and publications around the notion of 'home'. I have set up an art consultancy with another woman artist, Mimi Cuthbert, based on the idea of integrating art into 'everyday' life. Our exhibitions have been presented in the living environment of the home, so artworks mix in with other familiar objects in the kitchen, bathroom, dining room, playroom, bedroom, my study and office space. The house is open on certain days so the public can wander around seeing the work *in situ*. We have focused particularly on performance and live art which, by its nature, allows us to treat the audience as guests. We also use the Web to document our projects and present live Webcasts, which keep our work visible when the house is not open to the public. We have had an enormous response to 'home' and much interest from the media – possibly an indication of the general interest in bringing the spheres of work and home together. It is also true that huge numbers of artists, both male and female, now create work on childhood memories, the domestic, gender and the body, making 'home' a highly relevant and vital environment in which to present and contexualise work.

On a personal level, these new initiatives move me away from the isolated artist working in her studio and allow me to work in more flexible ways, maximising my time. It is about having the confidence to imagine myself as an artist, establishing a new model for myself, setting my own agenda and priorities. I am hopeful that I have found a way to continue my art while asserting the importance of being a mother.

PJ Crook
Portrait of the Artist Watching Her Children Grow

My mother tells me that even as a baby I made marks on the walls and would paint on them with any material that came to hand. I have often wondered whether it was during my two-year separation from her at the age of seven, while she was recovering from tuberculosis, that I developed the ability to travel through my mind's eye, working out ways to get back to my mother. As an adult, my own dual roles of mother and artist are so closely entwined they seem to stem from the same source. Although not always consciously, I have kept a visual chronicle of my children's progress through their infancy, childhood and adolescence. Usually working from memory and often in retrospect, the paintings are frequently overlaid with reminiscences of my own childhood and even sometimes with stories of when my parents were young.

The question of whether or not to be a mother never really occurred to me; in fact, motherhood itself started my journey as a painter. There are women who make the choice not to bear children, feeling that they will be able to devote themselves totally to their artistic endeavour, and perhaps agreeing with Cyril Connolly's verdict that 'There is no more sombre enemy of good art than the pram in the hall.' (*Enemies of Promise*, G. Routledge & Sons, 1938.)

However, I am not convinced. I have a feeling that

choosing to exclude other areas of experience might induce a more introspective view of life that does not always enhance or facilitate creative output. If an artist becomes too self-conscious or analytical of their work it can impede progress and growth. It is true that I have barely had time to draw breath while fitting my work in and around the needs of my children and my family life, including the care of my mother, my late father and also my partner Richard's father. I have not had time to read as much as childless artists or to question my work as often. But my work and career have developed to such a degree that I now exhibit internationally, holding shows with my dealers in London, Paris, New York, Florida and Toronto. Artist friends are always surprised by the huge amount of work that flows out of my studio in the form of exhibitions and commissions. Early on in my career I would impose deadlines on myself by entering competitive and open exhibitions; now deadlines arise of their own volition! Limited time has made me learn to be decisive, which has benefited my creativity.

I have known women who became martyrs to motherhood and marriage, stifling their own creative and intellectual potential. Unable to harness this energy in tandem with caring for their young, they often channelled it through them. There are others who have hidden behind this mantle as an excuse for not using their talent, fearing the risk of failure.

Motherhood is perhaps the ultimate primal creative process and the human gestation period is similar in many ways to the fertile mind, where ideas are incubated and burgeon forth when they are fully formed. It is not without good reason that artists' works are frequently referred to as their children –

how often have people asked me if I feel a sadness at parting from my paintings. During each of my two pregnancies I found that all my energy was used in nurturing and getting ready for the birth and care of the baby I bore within my womb. In the same way the germ of an idea manifests itself within the psyche, growing ever bigger within the mind's eye, and is transferred onto the canvas or structure that the artist is bringing to fruition. For me it is this process rather than the glory of exhibiting the final piece that is most fulfilling. Like the children making their own way in the world, eventually these paintings continue their existence elsewhere.

Although in my teens I had studied at art school for five years and knew in my heart that I was a painter or sculptor, my career did not follow a straight line. During one college holiday I worked at a local printers where the young graphic designer, an ex-student from the same college, questioned me about the wisdom of training in fine art. How was I going to make a living? It was rare to do so unless one taught. This argument seemed to make sense, so I changed my specialisation from painting and sculpture to textile design and printmaking. After graduation I set off to London where I freelanced as a textile designer, then set up in business with a fellow student who later became my husband and the children's father. We were designing and manufacturing all manner of pop art objects, including toys and jewellery.

Much of my work is now large and three-dimensional, but the shape it took, especially in those early days, was very much dictated by the circumstances under which I created. I had always felt a strong pull towards sculpture as a student and deciding in which direction to go was something of a dilemma. With restricted space and time I felt that chipping away at large blocks of stone or mixing buckets of plaster in the kitchen would have proved much too noisy, dangerous and impractical with small children about. Painting on a small scale was almost silent and enabled me to keep a listening ear.

After the birth of Henrietta, my first child, I realised that if I didn't start to paint then there might always be an excuse not to do so; I decided that when I finished breast-feeding her at six months I would begin to paint for a short space of time each evening after I had put her to bed, even if it was only half an hour. Working at the kitchen table, little by little, I began to learn anew. I was painting on tiny pieces of board often measuring no more than six by four inches, but it was an exciting time of experimentation and discovery.

Three years after Henrietta, Nathan, my second child, was born. The images I created during these early years seemed to relate to the children themselves, and often reflected the bedtime stories I would tell them. As my children grew and prospered, so too did my work, the paintings increasing in size and confidence. During this time I learned to work in artificial light and to concentrate for long periods of time. These acquired skills have proved invaluable when exhibition deadlines draw near and often sustain me right through the night.

In 1995 I took part in a drama documentary for TV, based on the life of Bristol-born artist Rolinda Sharples (1793–1838), played by Toyah Willcox. Both the director, Lee Cox and the writer, Hazel Gower were art-school-trained women who juggled their creative careers with bringing up three children each, while Toyah had made the decision not to have children. Rolinda's parents were both artists, her mother having been one of her father's students. They moved from Bristol to America while she was a child, where her father made a series of portraits of the founders of the new republic. His young wife Ellen then made copies of these, which helped earn them a handsome living. With such an example, it might seem strange that when she returned to Bristol with her mother after her father's death, Rolinda decided firmly against motherhood and marriage. A husband would absorb too much of her energy and time and the risk of dying in childbirth seemed too great. Her subject matter was sometimes controversial; it was not really considered proper for a woman to make social comment through her work. Flower paintings and portraits were acceptable but Rolinda tackled themes such as *Observations of a Court Martial*, *Stoppage at the Bank* and *Racecourse Scenes*; subjects that were difficult for her to sell or exhibit. Sadly Rolinda died of breast cancer in her forties and was outlived by her mother, who founded the Royal West of England Academy in 1849.

In the film I play myself, and my opportunities are contrasted with Rolinda's situation. I am able to combine work with motherhood and have a partner who helps and encourages me (he also does the cooking). I can tackle subject matter that is often uncomfortable, such as the series of works I made during the Gulf war. *Other Mothers' Sons* (Imperial War Museum) was created out of fear and empathy for the mothers who had nurtured and protected young men through infancy and childhood, only to risk losing them in a battle that was not of their making. The work itself shows row upon row of multinational soldiers in camouflage, undulating on a corrugated surface which, when one walks past, conveys a feeling of movement. It is a visual requiem. Another work in the same series, *Writing on the Wall*, shows a portrait of a man in a gas mask with tombstone-like figures fleeing in the background. I had been moved by reports of families in Israel having to wear gas masks during the Scud missile attacks and it struck me that for an infant to see their parents changed into these strange elephantine creatures would be horrendous.

In *Writing on the Wall*, I looked at the paternal. A more recent painting, the very large polyptych, *Fin de Siècle*, painted during the Kosovo conflict, focuses on that closest and most intimate of relationships, the mother and child. I make reference to the tradition of religious icons, particularly the image of the Madonna and Child which for two millennia has held such an important place in Western art. This vision of motherhood has, over the centuries, depicted the ideal of unconditional and tender love. The Madonna in my painting is shown wearing her traditional blue, a colour also often associated with the nursing sister, but is again transformed into a disturbing and surreal figure by the addition of the gas mask.

A mother's greatest fear is that anything should harm the children she loves. Those mothers whose sons made the ultimate sacrifice, losing their lives fighting for their country or their beliefs, know the anguish the Madonna must also have suffered. The infant in *Fin de Siècle* makes reference to the Christchild and is also symbolic of the new century and a world which is under constant threat, not only from war and famine but also pollution and disregard for our natural resources, wildlife and fellow human beings. Again, in the tradition of religious painting, there is always the presence of hope and peace, seen in the upper section of the work a white dove (frequently the symbol for the Holy Spirit or, as in Chagall and Picasso, a symbol of peace); whereas the crows, living off carrion, are often used to evoke the fear of death and its aftermath (as in Van Gogh's late paintings and Hammer Horror films).

One of the great advantages of having a career as a painter is the possibility of working from home, thus combining the living space for family life with my studio. Unlike Augustus John's children who were expected to knock at the door before entering, my children have always been included in my studio, seeing it as part of the home (although sometimes when they visited with small friends, I suspected that little additions had been made to my work). My children probably thought that it was the norm to have a mum who was an artist and that all mothers painted. The flexibility of a work/home environment was enormous, I could adapt my working hours to fit around the children – if they were unwell or away from school I could work at night after they were asleep and I was always in earshot when needed.

After my first marriage broke up, my creativity became a lifeline and I was fortunate in that it also became our financial support. The works gradually grew not only in their number and scale but also in the income they provided. I did not feel, as many working mothers do, a sense of guilt that the children missed out in any way. I was able to avoid the need for complex arrangements involving a nanny or child-minders. The children and my creativity always seemed to be part of the same whole – a way of life, fulfilling and rounded. On the occasions when I did need help, it would be my own mother who provided it, thereby helping to nurture her own child's creativity.

However, this way of life does have some disadvantages. It is rarely apparent to other people that a woman who is at home bringing up her children could also be at work. Although they are usually very interested in what I do, some seem to view it as a hobby rather than a career, after all, most people have a friend or relation who paints. If I had gone out to work in an office, people would not be able to intrude into my working hours. So, I have had to develop the knack of declining invitations to coffee or similar functions during school time. But it is still hard for others to resist dropping in, knowing that I am at home. Even a short interruption can break a train of thought that perhaps may never be rekindled. I have also had to learn how to ignore unnecessary housework, although at times it would be much easier than trying to summon up the energy to create out of nothing by making the first tentative marks on a pristine white canvas.

The children's very presence has provided me with great inspiration. Because their faces are so near and dear to me, they appear in my work, even when I had not necessarily recognised them as the protagonists within a story, others would point out either the physical resemblance or the way they 'felt' like them. Among my earliest small works was one of a young girl, aged perhaps five or six, which was painted while Henrietta was not even one year old, but which bore an almost exact resemblance to the way she looked when she got to that age. Whether this was a premonition or me fashioning the child to my vision of her I cannot tell.

My anxiety too would often translate on to the canvas. Once, when both children were away from me – Nathan on a French exchange in Annecy and Henrietta in Florence and Rome with my sister – two paintings emerged. The first, called *The Terrible Twins* shows the central figure of a woman holding the reins of two small infants, each one tugging in a different direction – the boy climbing on a chair towards the open window and the girl pulling towards the door which is ajar. The second of the two works again shows the infants this time playing with toys, totally oblivious to the ominous shadow of a figure through the doorway. But in through the window flies the guardian angel to watch over them and keep them safe. The paintings were to form part of the exhibition I was working on. My New York dealer, who was staging it, found the photographs of these works so disturbing that she telephoned to say she didn't feel she could include them. I was furious and told her that they were part of me and stemmed from the same place as all the other works. Eventually she capitulated. Both works were sold to the same woman collector before the show had even opened.

My subject matter is wide and diverse, drawing on my observations of others, including my father and his passion for gambling. But central to it all is motherhood, providing inspiration for works such as *Portrait of the Artist Watching Her Two Children Grow* (Cheltenham Art Gallery & Museum). In this,

I peer through the door to one side of the composition, into an interior which although not exactly like our own family living room, has such a similar feel that people think it is a portrait of that very room. Playing with time, I show the children at several stages in their lives, held together at one moment, and starting with the infant Nathan on the floor with his building bricks. Then a tiny Henrietta, aged four in her first school uniform, and again slightly older in a tutu; like many little girls she loved to dance and is shown manipulating a marionette, much as parents' lives are dictated by the needs of their children. Meanwhile, Nathan, in a sailor suit, plays the violin. Although Nathan did not have a sailor suit, but my father did, and the painting makes reference to his childhood too – reflections of the grandfather in the son. I show the children again, this time in their mid-teens almost fully grown. To the left-hand side of the painting Nathan stands, wearing the red and white striped waistcoat I had made for him to wear when performing with the Punch and Judy puppets he is holding. He had carved these from lime wood and had performed with them since the age of ten, becoming the youngest professor in the Punch and Judy Fellowship. At eleven he appeared in the Glyn Edwards television film *As Pleased as Punch*. I used his Punch and Judy puppets within the painting both for their personal associations and because, in their grotesque way of battling with each other over the baby, they mimic an uncomfortable version of family life. The family group reflected in the mirror central to the painting shows me playing the piano (a wish fulfilment) with my parents and partner Richard, who had some years ago decided to become a father to the children, nurturing their creativity and my own.

In retrospect, it is interesting to observe that my paintings have grown in scale and ambition at a similar rate to the growth of my children, who have both become art students. They are now very much taller than me (I am barely five foot tall) and my works also tower and loom above me, often reaching from floor to ceiling. As the children have become independent and travelled so too have the works. Outgrowing their home, they now require more space: I am about to start going out to work, having bought the house opposite for this very purpose.

Silvia Ebert
The Joy of the Dance

I would not categorise dancing as a creative art –
anyhow not as I practised it, as a professional. It is an
interpretative art. The dancer is completely in the
hands of the choreographer, who is, hopefully, trying
to interpret the music. The choreographer may use
improvisation, working closely with her dancers to
create steps and movements that suit their physical
and emotional styles or, as in classical ballet, the steps
may have been passed down by word of mouth over
generations and been interpreted and sometimes
altered to suit the dancer of the moment. The *corps de
ballet* should ideally be clones of one another: all
swans turning their heads as one, all moving their
arms or legs identically. There is absolutely no room
in the *corps de ballet* for creation or even interpreta-
tion. Only the joy of dancing in perfect harmony with
the music and the other dancers.

That said, the joy of dancing and expressing myself
in this way was very important to me for many years.
When I could escape from family responsibilities and
dance professionally (under the name Silvia Ashmole)
it was like drinking at the fountain of life: I was
refreshing my own spirit. Also, because the experience
was squeezed into a busy schedule, it was like a treat,
a joyous flight. Many performers find it difficult to
wind down after a show; they are on such an

adrenalin high they find it hard to relax. I must say, with the pure physical exertion of looking after a family, training and performing, I never had this difficulty!

During my training – this is all fifty-five years ago now – my sights were firmly set on classical ballet. I resented having to attend tap, ballroom and musical comedy classes which formed part of the broad-based and excellent curriculum at the school I attended (The Ripman School, later amalgamated with the Cone School and renamed Arts Educational). I enjoyed the modern dance classes (Laban Method), so-called 'Greek Dancing', drama and of course, the classical ballet classes. My first professional job was in *Sigh No More*, an 'Intimate Revue'[1] by Noël Coward. Shortly before the run ended I auditioned and was accepted for the Royal Ballet. Covent Garden Opera House had been completely renovated after the war and the Ballet, taking on a few extra dancers, went into it with a beautiful production of the *Sleeping Beauty* designed by Oliver Messel.

When I joined the Royal Ballet I thought that all my dreams had come true. However, I found the structure of the Ballet not at all conducive to a happy working atmosphere. To start with, there was a very high proportion of girls and very few men! (Especially then, when all young men had to serve in the forces.) The soloists were a world apart and the *corps de ballet* were continuously competing with one another for the smaller roles. The older dancers, who had been with the company for many years, resented the intake of very young, keen dancers straight out of school. Ninette de Valois was a pretty formidable and very authoritarian character and we were all quite frightened of her. At the end of the eight-month season I left the company, bitterly disappointed. However, I was lucky enough to audition for and be accepted by the Ballet Theatre of New York for their London season at Covent Garden. There I was able to dance under much happier circumstances and also to see the new ballets the Americans brought with them: choreographers such as Jerome Robbins, Michael Kidd, and Balanchine and Agnes de Mille, with whom I later worked. This was like a breath of fresh air to me. The war had meant that British audiences had missed all the developments in modern dance that had taken place on the other side of the Atlantic. The company seemed to express an optimism and energy quite different from the English style, which I still find a bit insipid and lacking in temperament at times.

I was never a highly technical dancer and so would probably not have got out of the *corps* of the Royal Ballet. As it was, because I was expressive and musical, I had a very varied and interesting career, sometimes with small speaking parts, in intimate revue, films, musicals, cabaret and opera. It was probably because I was so flexible that I was able to continue with my career and combine it with having a family. I did not not have to train for two hours every day to keep the shine on a virtuoso technique, but concentrated on expression. (In fact, I find that many small ballet companies have today become so obsessed with technique and athleticism – which can be amazing in their own way – that the performances have become somewhat sterile.)

I have been extremely lucky with my body. I only decided that I would like to become a dancer, when I was sixteen and had never done any dancing before. I was tested by a ballet teacher for suitability and she found that I was extremely loose and had a natural 'turn out' so that the classical positions of the feet and legs wouldn't present serious problems. As I was starting my training so late this was very important. My parents were both slim, healthy, full of energy and self-discipline, and these characteristics were thankfully passed on to me.

Because of my strong tummy muscles, my first baby did not start showing until I stopped dancing, which was at seven months. (I was performing in *Carousel* at Drury Lane Theatre.) When Tobias was a month old I took him in his cradle (no carry-cots then) on buses and trains from Blackheath to the West End to go to my ballet classes. Then I was accepted to dance at Glyndebourne. My husband husband Peter and I, lived with Tobias in rooms in the village nearby. The company car (an ancient Rolls-Royce) would come and pick us up in time for rehearsal during which I would put Tobias out in the Glyndebourne garden where he slept peacefully until lunchtime. I fed him, changed him and put him down for the afternoon.

Once the performance began, I placed Tobias's cot in a small dressing room at stage level. It was soon christened the nappy room and I can remember standing on stage in a crowd scene and the message being passed to me, 'Where are the clean nappies?' I also remember the choreographer was shocked, once, to discover me in horrific tow wig and blacked out teeth – witch make-up for the opera – suckling an amazingly beautiful, brown, chubby baby. Of course, it was a very demanding routine. I had to wash nappies and baby clothes in the dressing-room washbasin and also fit in time to play with my child.

He soon became a little mascot for the performers and even made an appearance in one scene when the opera was televised.

My second son, Charles, was born fourteen months after the first. During the pregnancy I was sick a lot and a hiatus-hernia was diagnosed. Because of this I was told that I should not have any more babies, but the following six pregnancies went completely smoothly! In fact, if someone said 'Silvia, you do look well!' I would think 'Aha' and check my dates. I am thankful to my first gyneacologist who told me to continue living as 'normal' during pregnancy: if I was used to doing wild modern dancing or tarantellas or standing on a high ladder painting ceilings, I should go on doing it. I was able to keep dancing during my pregnancies and believe this was one reason I kept so well.

Another reason I did not stop dancing was that we needed the money. After the birth of my second child, Peter's first wife sent her two little girls to live with us, so now we had four children. I absolutely had to dance at Glyndebourne that summer as our finances were precarious: and although my earnings were not high, they were a help. So we got an au-pair and three weeks after Charles's birth I started training.

After a few weeks our au-pair caught scarlet fever and was put into an isolation hospital. I had to send the little girls back to their mother for the interim and I coped with the two babies, aged two months and sixteen months, between extremely demanding rehearsals for *Alceste*. I lost a stone in a week and was painfully thin. It was a very difficult summer, but I have lovely memories of it too. The babies were angelic and healthy and the dancing was absolutely my style. Things got easier when I was dancing in the West End. Because my work was mostly in the evening I had lots of time to care for my little ones. Problems only arose if I was involved in anything that had a lot of matinées, such as the time when I was playing the Fairy in the Palladium Pantomime, *Cinderella* (with Julie Andrews, Max Bygraves and Richard Hearne).

Somehow, I managed to time my babies so that I could dance every summer at Glyndebourne, but after moving to Hanover in Germany, where Peter was chief opera producer at the State Theatre, there were no opportunities to work during the winter. It also became increasingly difficult, as the family grew, to divide my attention between husband, children and career. Sometimes I felt torn in three directions. Peter was always very supportive of my career but it was a different ball game in the 1950s and 1960s. Peter was the chief breadwinner and at the time it was taken for granted that a man's career should take precedence. (When I see how involved our sons and sons-in-law are with childcare and housework, it strikes me how far the women's movement has come in the last fifty years!) When Peter started doing productions all over the world there was always the question of whether I could join him for at least part of the four- to six-week period. We were lucky in that we were occasionally able to leave Peter's aunt in charge of the children so that I could go away for short periods.

Gradually my career tapered off. I didn't really regret this as I had been able to continue dancing for a long time. In my last professional engagement, the opera *Macbeth*, I was seven months pregnant with my seventh child (would it be possible for a dancer to do this today, I wonder?)

For me motherhood was also a wonderfully creative experience: I found self-expression through making a home for my family, in travelling to many different places and discovering the world with my children. If you are a creative person that creativity will naturally emerge in some way. For me these experiences were not only enjoyable but also of the utmost importance. The virgin territory of your child's mind is so precious: what you write on it will shape their whole future.

But motherhood also changed me as a dancer. I found greater self-confidence, more aggression (defending my cubs), and also completely unselfish love. These things added enormously to the expressiveness of my dancing. When you have felt the indescribable joy after the birth of a child, you know joy on a different level. When you have been through the agony of worrying over a seriously ill child, you have looked into new depths. Through your child's eyes you see things in a fresh light. You may, through your child's questions, have to explore your own beliefs. This enriches you as a person and as a performer.

All the same, dance had meant an escape, and without it the vagaries of our family life, the long separations and the need to be emotionally giving all the time, did result in my becoming rather stressed at one stage.

Later in life I experienced the pleasure of teaching my own daughters when I was asked to take over the village ballet class in Sussex. When one of them graduated to a professional ballet company I attended all her premieres. I saw myself in her dancing, which was a great joy. There is no jealousy, for you have handed on the baton. Similarly with motherhood when you watch your children blossom into marvellous parents.

1. 'Intimate Revue' is a theatrical genre which is now more or less extinct. The name refers to the contrast with the lavish, spectacular revues seen on Broadway at that time. The show consisted of about fourteen separate items with dance numbers, songs, monologues and so on. Joyce Grenfell made her stage debut in *Sigh No More*.

Jacqueline Morreau
The Divided Self

How quickly one forgets the longueurs of motherhood the moment-to-moment concentration mothering demands. Time stands still. So much attention is required for the many details of children's lives. I rediscovered the slow pace of childcare time when I helped my older daughter with her own children. 'Is it only nine o'clock?', I would think when we had done a hundred things that morning, and I was already tired. Beyond fatigue, the mother or the artist takes a deep breath and forges on. Love for the child is the spur for the mother, and the need to make is what goads the artist. Yet it is within these elongated time frames of mothering, or making art, that the most important outcomes of life occur. Children are tended, nurtured, loved, taught, gain independence. Pictures are created with full concentration.

If I had to assess my performance as a mother, I'd say that, in general, I was what is called in psychological terms 'good enough'. My first demand on myself was that I should listen to what the child said, as attentively as I could. I realised in raising my first child (who was an only child for ten years), that what he wanted to say was important. His first sentences told me that he had had an injection at nursery school, and that his arm hurt. 'This arm hurt me. This arm okay.' I saw that children will find language for their concerns, and that they tell the truth as they see it.

My first son was born when I was twenty, and I had to do menial jobs for some years to support the family. It gave me the opportunity to learn about the underside of the world and to mature in important ways. When my son was six, I left his father and returned to university fulltime to become a medical illustrator. As I still had to support us, I worked in the evenings and there was not much time for art.

Luckily, when I ended my own childhood at twenty I had already been provided with enough tools, incentives, family precedents and perceivable talent, to be taken seriously as an artist-to-be. I had been encouraged both at school and by my family, subsidised from an early age with private lessons and art classes, and I was able to take advantage of a good library at home. I was, by preference, a very solitary child and was allowed to go to the parks and swimming pools and the river by myself, summer and winter, absorbing the natural world at my own pace. So I was very fortunate in already having had not only an intensive formal art training, but also a year in Paris and New York with other artist friends, looking at pictures, living a somewhat 'bohemian' life and making my first experimental paintings.

When I married again, I had three more children. Sometimes I could only hope to be a referee in their disputes with one another, as much as I tried to give them time and attention individually. The changing needs of each child were hard to focus on. The conflict between my own needs and protecting the children's growing space was very tiring, and the conflicts between them did not help. When I told them that later in life they would be grateful for having each other and would become friends, they didn't believe me. Luckily I spoke the truth; or it may have been a self-fulfilling prophecy. Now I am very proud of each of them, and despite any faults of their parents as parents they each live useful and creative lives.

As I look back, I see how desperate I was for a quiet moment to sit and stare. The first need of an artist is solitude. How can she find it within a ten- to twelve-hour working day, such as I had when I was a single, working mother and a mature student; or later with four children, a husband, a household, friends, relations? Every moment counted. I always carried a sketch book with me, drawing or writing notes on the train, observing people on the bus, drawing during the countless hours passed in doctors' waiting rooms or the school playground.

In 1968 we moved from Berkely, California to Lexington, Massachusetts, a commuter suburb for Cambridge and Boston, and in the early 1970s I began to show my work. Although it was reviewed and received well, I could still see that women's work was not very welcome in the commercial galleries, and that the work I did would not reach an audience because of both its proto-feminist and political subject matter and its figurative style.

Lexington felt like 'Stepford Wives' territory – the plastic smiles, the hidden dysfunctions. We were a family which didn't care much for appearances; we didn't have to care in California, where all our friends were creative, lateral-thinking people. In Lexington however I had to face the problem which many a creative woman must come to terms with: how to pass for normal in a society where there is an acceptance of conformity.

Some years later, the term 'global nomad' was coined to describe the displacement of families as the man moved from place to place for the good of his career. It described a condition of life which feminism began to address: the wife as an often unwilling appendage. If I had been aware of the universality of my situation I would have coped better. I might have recognised kindred spirits behind the smiles of some of the suburban wives. But as an artist – and a homesick one at that – I resisted. I tried as hard as I could to get through the day and still have a selfish moment or two. My children knew that I had this important secret life but of course they preferred it if I could pass for 'normal', so their friends and their parents would think we were 'the same'. My children recognised that I was often somewhere else when I was with them. They stopped asking what I was staring at, knowing that I was having an 'inner' moment. Or my children's friends would ask, 'Why does your mother look at me like that?' to which my younger son would say, 'Oh, she's only working out how she would draw you.'

I was not entirely alone in my oddity. I had a friend near by who was a deeply addicted alcoholic, but her children covered up for her brilliantly. I always felt that my children had a similar task. Yet my alcoholic friend and I still had to do all the things that have to be done – shopping, cooking, attending to family needs. She fumbled and stumbled literally, but I also needed much conscious effort to fulfil tasks most people accomplish with ease.

Above all, I had to guard my working time. I had to find ways to avoid social events: the chats, the coffees, the volunteer work, even neighbourliness. As soon as the door closed on the last child going off to school I left the dishes and the chaos, and went to my studio. Even when my children were very little I found a small office, somebody's shed, anywhere to be alone with my self and my work, if only for an hour or two. When they came home from school, I washed the breakfast dishes, we went shopping, I cooked and did any other neglected tasks. I learned all the time-saving tricks, like having a large box behind the sofa in which to collect all the chaos before supper, so that a superficial order prevailed.

'The soul selects her own society, then shuts the door' as Emily Dickinson wrote from her own experience. Many mothers find time for themselves through sleeplessness or, when sleeping, have revealing dreams. That clever dreamlife works away helping the artist. Artists also learn to concentrate during moments of snatched time. I can make a drawing or think through a problem – or just be open to thoughts that come unbidden – when suddenly the house is empty and I know there is a half-hour or more of uninterrupted time. It is true that for women artist who are mothers, working time is often fragmented, but the years of childrearing are not long in absolute terms. There is life after motherhood, as older mothers tell younger ones. A sculptor friend said to me, 'Don't wish these years away, but enjoy them as much as you can, they pass so quickly.'

Being a mother made me angry about much that was going on in the world, especially war and the rumours of war. I worried about the effects of nuclear testing on our children's generation and identified with the Vietnam mothers trying to protect their offspring. I felt that there were two ways for me to act: one was to bring those anxieties into my work, and the other was to take more action. So, although I preach solitude, I often joined whatever protests I could.

We moved to London in 1972, and I soon began to teach drawing at the Women's Art Alliance, and met artists involved in the women's movement. I think that without the women's movement, there would not have been opportunities for women artists to find expression for their own understanding of gender and politics, and certainly no opportunities to exhibit such work. Without the women's movement, none of the women we now celebrate would have had the support required to be so visible. From Louise Bourgeois to Rachel Whiteread to Paula Rego, none would have 'made it'. It took a revolutionary change in thinking about who can speak and who can be heard to make this possible. For most women artists of my generation, the ground-breaking text was Linda Nochlin's essay 'Why Have There Been No Great Women Artists?'[1] It passed from artist to artist, starting many discussions and heated arguments.

When the members I worked with at the Alliance called for action to expose the fact that women artists were almost totally absent from view in Great Britain, we spent time and energy trying to find a way towards changing this. Viewed dispassionately, one could say that helping to create a constituency of women artists, video makers, performance artists and so forth, which took at least five years of my life, was in my own interest. It was, and it worked. Many women were working in the same way, like Stephanie Dowrick who founded the Women's Press. However, when the women who worked on the planning of the exhibition, 'Women's Images of Men' (Catherine Elwes, Joyce

Agee, Pat Whiteread and myself) used to meet in the unheated rooms of the Women's Arts Alliance, or in Pat Whiteread's basement, it was also time carved out of family life, and our own practice. When we wrote the book, *Women's Images of Men* with Sarah Kent, describing what we had done and why, at least we could do it at home![2]

During the time when we were plotting the exhibitions and the season of events to go with them, I discovered a studio with terrific light, and as soon as I took the financial plunge, enough illustration work came my way to pay for it. My children were now in their teens and had their own busy lives so I worked all the hours I could. Fuelled by feminism and anger, I produced some of my best works.

Yes, in those years much of my work was definitely fuelled by rage at world events: much of it was therefore about sexual politics and other political issues. I had the example of a mother's political art in the work of Käthe Kollwitz and protest art from the German expressionists, as well as Goya and Daumier. I was inspired by the other artists who participated in the 'Women's Images of Men' shows, especially Marisa Rueda, Sue Coe, Anna Maria Pacheco, and Liz Frink. Women writers were increasingly being published such as my friend, the poet Judith Kazantzis, and the writers Tillie Olsen and Adrienne Rich, both of whom participated in the events which accompanied the central exhibition at the ICA in 1980.

When 'Women's Images of Men' had run its course as a touring exhibition, media circus, and book, I locked myself away and turned to other, more interior work. I thought, 'If I only have ten more years I can make some good work.' It was then that I drew my younger daughter sitting on my bed with her boyfriend's head in her lap. I thought a lot about the way girls often choose a terrible, unsuitable, possibly charming rogue on whom to lavish their first serious love. I did it myself and was left holding the baby: and here was my daughter doing the same thing. I realised that the myth of Psyche and Eros encapsulated this phenomenon. For what is this huge overwhelming sexual desire but the force for procreation, represented by the god Eros and the human Psyche.

This insight inspired me to re-examine my own past, and to look in great detail at the meanings embedded in the myth. I worked with this and related myths for the following five years, painting, drawing, etching. Eventually I got to the stage where I had a West End gallery and was selling work which I had never imagined anyone would buy. I had never worked with selling in mind, and no one was more astonished than me, but when the recession came, and the gallery closed, I was not too unhappy. It meant I had no outside pressure, except teaching. Whatever artists claim, any gallery wants you to keep producing what you have already sold successfully. They don't really want you to experiment with new work which might not find a buyer.

By this time, 1991, my children were all living in their own homes, though they would sometimes perch with us in the lean periods of their lives. They had all become very creative, each in his or her own way and had not reacted to my eccentricities by becoming more conventional.

When children leave home it is time to recover who you wanted to be, to re-examine your agenda, renew the relationship with your partner and reclaim your body, especially if you are no longer fertile! My next series of paintings celebrated my freedom, and my pleasure in my new role as artist and sensual being. 'Fold Upon Fold' is a series which combines notions of dreaming, sleeping, sexuality, and the sea. I related the movement of the sheets of a bed with the forms of waves as they encounter the shore. I wanted the work to have a sensuality I had not achieved before. However, while I was still working on these more abstract paintings I invited my younger daughter, Andrea, to come to work in the annex of my studio, which had just become free. The studio she had found for herself, in which she had that sacred solitude we all crave, was suddenly closed for demolition so, without really wanting to, she came to work in the extra space I had. It was an impossible situation for both of us, but at least we could laugh about it. She and I have been uncannily tuned into each other since she was born and when she began to work in my studio, ideas filtered through the walls: we began either to work on the same ideas, or avoid areas we thought the other was exploring.

If it was stressful for me, how much worse was it for her? I was the established artist, Andrea was just beginning. We had both hoped that her work would follow on from her film and video course. She had made witty and beautiful photo-collages and some wonderful short videos. She had always been as passionate about film as I am about painting but she lost her confidence when the equipment she'd had access to at college was no longer available. She faced the dilemma all new graduates face – where do I go from here?

It was around this time that I glimpsed two girls

trying to get into the same coat and recognised that this was what was happening to my daughter and me. I had used a heavy red coat as a symbol of identity in my very earliest feminist work, 'The Divided Self' series, which explored the conflicts between motherhood and art, desire and work, domesticity and the muse. And here was that coat again. This set me going, but where did it leave Andrea? We knew what her problem was, one that Freud had recognised too. But, however much you want to kill the parent and take over her identity, you won't solve the problem that way. The real answer, if you are to follow your parent's trade, is to be as good, and preferably better, than they are. 'It is a poor student who does not exceed his master.'

This was a conflict for me as well, but as the mother of this woman it would also be to my credit if she were to become a better artist than me. In fact, it would be a kind of extension of my own life: parents have always wanted children to exploit the family talents as it is wasteful, to say the least, if they do not. This work also made me think about my own mother, and remember that she had warned me how hard motherhood would be: 'Wait until you have your own children, then you'll know what it's like!' I explored the many aspects of this mother/daughter conflict through my next series of paintings and drawings. 'The Struggle for the Coat' invaded Andrea's territory insofar as she was partly the subject, but she was also working through the conflict in her own way.

The 'Struggle for the Coat' series continued in a difficult and often clumsy way. I felt compelled to do it, but often resented it. One night, after many versions I dreamed that my daughter and I were on stage, both confident and smartly dressed. I said 'Now we can both be beautiful' and woke up full of delight. For us, this dream provided a resolution. The series has proved to be a powerful symbolic work for many other women too, as they apply it to their own conflicts with mothers or sisters – anyone closely loved and yet threatening to their personal space and identity.

Throughout, my husband and the father of my younger three children, and stepfather to my older son, has been as enabling as anyone could be. He has supported my projects, looked after the children when he could, provided me with space to work, and above all, believed in me. He has been a father and mother to me as well as a husband. Most of my friends who have continued to make good work have had supportive partners; it would be far more difficult to sustain both motherhood and creativity without such support. Indeed in my years as an activist in the women's movement all the other conspirators had such support to a large extent.

As for children: the surprise of love, the energy it gives you to get up in the night, and in the morning, to do one more thing, for them, and then another and another; the demonstration of the inborn will to grow and learn that unfolds day after day the way a plant unfurls – all of this sustains you as an artist as well. At the same time my mother's warning was true. I did see what she saw – rebellion marking each stage of growth, the assertion of the self, trying to fashion one's own way. I too was often exasperated, exhausted, fed up. I would rush out of the house after the children's tearful goodbyes to arrive at my studio totally wrecked, needing an hour to reach that place where the work takes off.

Perhaps if I had not had children I would have had more worldly success. But I don't think so. Now I count each day I have energy and ideas as a wonderful gift. Looking back, I realise my older daughter is right to say that the period of childrearing that requires so much attention goes by very quickly and that its rewards are greater than the energy devoted to it, no matter how divided I felt at the time.

1   In Thomas B. Hess and Elizabeth Baker (eds), *Art and Sexual Politics*. New York: Macmillan, 1972.
2   Sarah Kent and Jacqueline Morreau (eds), London: *Writers and Readers*, 1985. Reprinted, Pandora, 1991.

Alice Walker
One Child of One's Own

A Meaningful Digression within the Work(s)

It is perfectly true that I, like many other women who work, especially as writers, was terrified of having children.

I feared being fractured by the experience if not overwhelmed. I thought the quality of my writing would be considerably diminished by motherhood – that nothing that was good for my writing could come out of having children.

My first mistake was in thinking 'children' instead of 'child'. My second was in seeing The Child as my enemy rather than the racism and sexism of an oppressive capitalist society. My third was in believing none of the benefits of having a child would accrue to my writing.

In fact, I had bought the prevailing sexist directive: you have to have balls (be a man) to write. In my opinion, having a child is easily the equivalent of having balls. In truth, it is more than equivalent: ballsdom is surpassed.

Someone asked me once whether I thought women artists should have children, and, since we were beyond discussing why this question is never asked artists who are men, I gave my answer promptly.

'Yes,' I said, somewhat to my surprise. And, as if to amend my rashness, I added: 'They should have children – *assuming this is of interest to them* – but only one.'

'Why only one?' this Someone wanted to know.

'Because with one you can move,' I said. 'With more than one you're a sitting duck.'

The year after my only child, Rebecca, was born, my mother offered me uncharacteristically bad advice: 'You should have another one soon,' said she, 'so that Rebecca will have someone to play with, and so you can get it all over with faster.'

Such advice does not come from what a woman recalls of her own experience. It comes from a pool of such misguidance women have collected over the millennia to help themselves feel less foolish for having more than one child. This pool is called, desperately, pitiably, 'Women's Wisdom'. In fact, it should be called 'Women's Folly'.

The rebellious, generally pithy advice that comes from a woman's own experience more often resembles my mother's automatic response to any woman she meets who pines for children but has been serenely blessed with none: 'If the Lord sets you free, be free indeed.' *This crafty justification of both non-conformity and a shameless revelling in the resultant freedom is what women and slaves everywhere and in every age since the Old Testament have appropriated from the Bible.*

'No thank you,' I replied. 'I will never have another child out of this body, again.'

'But why do you say that?' she asked breathlessly; perhaps stunned by my redundancy. 'You married a man who's a wonderful fatherly type. He has so much love in him he should have fifty children running around his feet.'

I saw myself sweeping them out from around his feet like so many ants. If they're running around his feet for the two hours between the time he comes home from the office and the time we put them to bed, I thought, they'd be underneath my desk all day. Sweep. Sweep.

My mother continued. 'Why,' she said, 'until my fifth child I was like a young girl. I could pick up and go anywhere I wanted to.' She *was* a young girl. She was still under twenty-five when her fifth child was born, my age when I became pregnant with Rebecca. Besides, since I am the last child in a family of eight, this image of nimble flight is not the one lodged for ever in my mind. I remember a woman struggling to get everyone else dressed for church on Sunday and only with the greatest effort being able to get ready on time herself. But, since I am not easily seduced by the charms of painful past experience, recalled in present tranquillity, I did not bring this up.

At the time my mother could 'pick up and go' with five children, she and my father travelled, usually, by wagon. I can see how that would have been pleasant: it is pleasant still in some countries – in parts of China, Cuba, Jamaica, Mexico, Greece, and other places. A couple of slow mules, ambling along a bright Southern road, the smell of pine and honeysuckle. absence of smog, birds chirping. Those five, dear little voices piping up in back of the wagon seat, healthy from natural foods. Plums! Bird! Tree! Flowers! Scuppernongs! Enchanting.

'The other reason I will never have another child out of this body is because having a child *hurts*, even more than toothache (and I am sure no one who has had toothache but not childbirth can imagine this), and it changes the body.'

Well, there are several responses from the general supply of Women's Folly my mother could have chosen to answer this. She chose them all.

'*That* little pain,' she scoffed *(although, caught in a moment of weakness, she has let slip that during my very own birth the pain was so severe she could not speak, not even to tell the midwife I had been born, and that because of the pain she was sure she would die – a thought that no doubt, under the circumstances, afforded relief. Instead, she blacked out, causing me to be almost smothered by the bedclothes).* 'That pain is over before you know it.' That is response number one. Number two is, 'The thing about that *kind* of pain is that it does a funny thing to a woman [*Uh-oh, I thought, this is going to be the Women's Folly companion to the women-sure-are-funny-creatures stuff*]; looks like the more it hurts you to give birth, the more you love the child.' (Is *that* why she loves me so much, I wonder. Naturally, I had wanted to be loved for myself, not for her pain.) Number three: 'Sometimes the pain, *they say*, isn't even real. Well, not as real as it feels at the time.' (This one deserves comment made only with blows, and is one of the reasons women sometimes experience muscle spasms around their mothers.) And then, number four, the one that angers me most of all: 'Another thing about the pain, *you soon forget it.*'

Am I mistaken in thinking I have never forgotten a pain in my life? Even those at parties, I remember.

'I remember every moment of it perfectly,' I said. 'Furthermore, I don't like stretch marks. I hate them, especially on my thighs' (which are otherwise gorgeous, and of which I am vain). Nobody had told me that my body, after bearing a child, would not be the same. I had heard things like: 'Oh, your figure, and especially your breasts [of which I am also vain] will be better than ever.' They sagged.

Well, why did I have a child in the first place?

Curiosity. Boredom. Avoiding the draft. Of these three reasons, I am redeemed only by the first. Curiosity is my natural state and has led me headlong into every worthwhile experience (never mind the others) I have ever had. It justifies itself. Boredom, in my case, means a lull in my writing, emotional distance from whatever political movement I am involved in, inability to garden, read, or daydream – easily borne if there are at least a dozen good movies around to attract me. Alas, in Jackson, Mississippi, where my husband, Mel, and I were living in 1968, there were few. About the draft we had three choices: the first, conscientious objector status for Mel, was immediately denied us, as was 'alternative service to one's country', which meant, in his case, desegregating Mississippi; the second was to move to Canada, which did not thrill me but which I would gladly have done rather than have Mel go to prison (Vietnam was never one of our choices); the third was, if Mel could not become twenty-six years old in time, to make of him 'a family man'.

From my journal, July 1968:
And now we own our house. For a brief time, surely.
And if the draft calls before I am certified pregnant,
what will we do? Go to Canada? Mel hates running
as much as I do, which is why we're in Mississippi. I

hate this country, but that includes being made to leave it...

January 2, 1969 [two months before I became pregnant]:
Only two and a half months until Mel is 26. If we can make it without having to 'flee ' the country, we will be thankful. I still think his draft board has a nerve asking him to join the Army. He's already in the Army.

My bad days were spent in depression, anxiety, rage against the war, and a state of apprehension over the amount of annual rainfall in Vancouver, and the slow rate of racial 'progress' in Mississippi. (Politicians were considered 'progressive' if they announced they were running for a certain office as candidates 'for *all* the people'; this was a subtle, they thought, announcement to blacks that their existence was acknowledged.) I was also trying to become pregnant.

My good days were spent teaching, writing a simple history book for use in black childcare centres in Jackson, recording black women's autobiographies, making a quilt (African fabrics, Mississippi string pattern), completing my second book, a novel – and trying to become pregnant.

Three days after I finished the novel, Rebecca was born. The pregnancy: the first three months I vomited. The middle three I felt fine and flew off to look at ruins in Mexico. The last three I was so big at 170 pounds I looked like someone else, which did not please me.

What is true about giving birth is...that it is miraculous. It might even be the one genuine miracle in life (which is, by the way, the basic belief of many 'primitive' religions). The 'miracle' of nonbeing, death, certainly pales, I would think, beside it. So to speak.

For one thing, though my stomach was huge and the baby (?!) constantly causing turbulence within it, I did not believe a baby, a person, would come out of me. I mean, look what had gone *in*. (Men have every right to be envious of the womb. I'm envious of it myself, and I have one.) But there she was, coming out, a long black curling lock of hair the first part to be seen, followed by nearly ten pounds of – a human being! Reader, I *stared*.

But this hymn of praise I, anyhow, have heard before, and will not permit myself to repeat, since there are, in fact, very few variations, and these have become boring and shopworn. They were boring and shopworn even at the birth of Christ, which is no doubt why 'Virgin Birth' and 'Immaculate Conception' were all the rage.

The point was, I was changed for ever. From a woman whose 'womb' had been, in a sense, her head – that is to say, certain small seeds had gone in, and rather different if not larger or better 'creations' had come out – to a woman who . . . had two wombs! No. To a woman who had written books, conceived in her head, and who had also engendered at least one human being in her body. In the vast general store of '*literary* Women's Folly' I discovered these warnings: 'Most women who wrote in the past were childless' – Tillie Olsen. Childless and *white*, I mentally added. 'Those Lady Poets must not have babies, man,' John Berryman, a Suicide Poet himself, is alleged to have said. Then, from 'Anonymous', so often a woman who discourages you, 'Women have not created as fully as men because once she has a child a woman cannot give herself to her work the way a man can...'

Well, I wondered, with great fear (and resentment against all this bad news), where is the split in me now? What is the damage? *Am I done for?* So much of 'Women's Folly', literary and otherwise, makes us feel constricted by experience rather than enlarged by it. Curled around my baby, feeling more anger and protectiveness than love, I thought of at least two sources of Folly Resistance 'Women's Folly' lacks. It lacks all conviction that women have the ability to plan their lives for periods longer than nine months, and it lacks the courage to believe that experience, and the expression of that experience, may simply be different, unique even, rather than 'greater' or 'lesser'. The art or literature that saves our lives *is great to us*, in any case; more than that, as a Grace Paley character might say, we do not need to know.

It helped tremendously that by the time Rebecca was born I had no doubts about being a writer. (Doubts about making a *living* by writing, always.) Write I did, night and day, *something*, and it was not even a choice, as having a baby was a choice, but a necessity. When I didn't write I thought of making bombs and throwing them. Of shooting racists. Of doing away – as painlessly and neatly as possible (except when I indulged in Kamikaze tactics of rebellion in my daydreams) – with myself. Writing saved me from the sin and *inconvenience* of violence – as it saves most writers who live in 'interesting' oppressive times and are not afflicted by personal immunity.

I began to see, during a period when Rebecca and I were both ill – we had moved to New England for a

year and a half because I needed a change from
Mississippi – that her birth, and the difficulties it
provided us, joined me to a body of experience and a
depth of commitment to my own life hard to
comprehend otherwise. Her birth was the
incomparable gift of seeing the world at quite a
different angle than before, and judging it by
standards that would apply far beyond my natural
life. It also forced me to understand, viscerally,
women's need for a store of 'Women's Folly', and yet
feel on firm ground in my rejection of it. But rejection
also has its pain.

Distance is required, even now.

**Of a ghastly yet useful joint illness, which teacheth
our pilgrim that her child might be called in this world
of trouble the least of her myriad obstacles –**

*Illness has always been of enormous benefit to me. It
might even be said that I have learned little from
anything that did not in some way make me sick.*

The picture is not an unusual one: a mother and small
child, new to the harshness of the New England winter
in the worst flu wave of the century. The mother, flat on
her back with flu, the child, burning with fever and
whooping cough. The mother calls a name someone has
given her, a famous pediatrician – whose popular
writings reveal him to be sympathetic, witty, something
of a feminist, even – to be told curtly that she should not
call him at his home at any hour. Furthermore, he does
not make house calls of any kind, and all of this is
delivered in the coldest possible tone.

Still, since he is the only pediatrician she knows of
in this weird place, she drags herself up next morning,

when temperatures are below zero and a strong wind is blasting off the river, and takes the child to see him. He is scarcely less chilly in person, but, seeing she is black, makes a couple of liberal comments to put her at her ease. She hates it when his white fingers touch her child.

A not unusual story. But it places mother and child for ever on whichever side of society is opposite this man. She, the mother, begins to comprehend on deeper levels a story she wrote years before she had a child, of a black mother, very poor, who, worried to distraction that her child is dying and no doctor will come to save him, turns to an old folk remedy, 'strong horse tea'. Which is to say, horse urine. The child dies, of course.

Now too the mother begins to see new levels in the stories she is at that moment – dizzy with fever – constructing: Why she says, slapping her forehead, all History is current; all injustice continues on some level, somewhere in the world. 'Progress' affects few. Only revolution can affect many.

It was during this same period that, risen from her bed of pain, her child well again and adapting to the cold, the mother understood that her child, a victim of society as much as she herself – and more of one because as yet she was unable to cross the street without a guiding hand – was in fact the very least of her obstacles in her chosen work. This was brought home to her by the following experience, which, sickening as it was, yet produced in her several desired and ultimately healthful results. One of which was the easy ability to dismiss all people who thought and wrote as if she, herself, did not exist. By 'herself' she of course meant multitudes, of which she was at any given time in history a mere representative.

Our young mother had designed a course in black women writers which she proceeded to teach at an upper-class, largely white, women's college (her students were racially mixed). There she shared an office with a white woman feminist scholar who taught poetry and literature. This woman thought black literature consisted predominantly of Nikki Giovanni, whom she had, apparently, once seen inadvertently on TV. Our young mother was appalled. She made a habit of leaving books by Gwendolyn Brooks, Margaret Walker, Toni Morrison, Nella Larsen, Paule Marshall, and Zora Neale Hurston face up on her own desk, which was just behind the white feminist scholar's. For the truly scholarly feminist, she thought, subtlety is enough. She had heard that this scholar was writing a massive study of women's imagination throughout the centuries, and what women's imaginations were better than those displayed on her desk, our mother wondered, what woman's imagination better than her own, for that matter; but she was modest and, as I have said, trusted to subtlety.

Time passed. The scholarly tome was published. Dozens of imaginative women paraded across its pages. They were all white. Papers of the status quo, like the *Times*, and liberal inquirers like the *New York Review of Books* and the *Village Voice*, and even feminist magazines such as *Ms.* (for which our young mother was later to work) actually reviewed this work with varying degrees of seriousness. Yet to our young mother, the index alone was sufficient proof that the work could not be really serious scholarship, only serious white female chauvinism. And for this she had little time and less patience.

In the prologue to her book, *The Female Imagination*, Patricia Meyer Spacks attempts to explain why her book deals solely with women in the 'Anglo-American literary tradition'. (She means, of course, *white* women in the Anglo-American literary tradition.) Speaking of the books she has chosen to study, she writes: 'Almost all delineate the lives of white middle-class women. Phyllis Chesler has remarked, "I have no theory to offer of Third World female psychology in America...As a white woman, I'm reluctant and unable to construct theories about experiences I haven't had." So am I: the books I talk about *describe familiar experience, belong to a familiar cultural setting*; their particular immediacy depends partly on these facts. My bibliography balances works everyone knows (*Jane Eyre*, *Middlemarch*) with works that should be better known (*The Story of Mary MacLane*). Still, the question remains: Why only these?' [my italics].

Why only these? Because they are white, and middle class, and because, to Spacks, female imagination is only that. Perhaps, however, this *is* the white female imagination, one that is 'reluctant *and unable* to construct theories about experiences I haven't had'. (Yet Spacks never lived in nineteenth-century Yorkshire, so why theorise about the Brontës?)

It took viewing 'The Dinner Party', a feminist statement in art by Judy Chicago, to illuminate the problem. In 1975 when her book, *Through the Flower*, was published, I was astonished, after reading it, to realize she knew nothing of black women painters. Not even that they exist. I was gratified therefore to learn that in 'The Dinner Party' there was a place 'set', as it were, for black women. The illumination came when I stood in front of it.

All the other plates are creatively imagined vaginas (even the one that looks like a piano and the one that bears a striking resemblance to a head of lettuce: and of course the museum guide flutters about talking of 'butterflies'!) The Sojourner Truth plate is the only one in the collection that shows – instead of a vagina – a face. In fact, *three* faces. One, weeping (a truly cliché tear), which 'personifies' the black women's 'oppression', and another, screaming (a no less cliché scream), with little ugly pointed teeth, 'her heroism', and a third, in gimcracky 'African' design, smiling; as if the African woman, pre-American slavery, or even today, had no woes.[1] (There is of course a case to be made for being 'personified' by a face rather than a vagina, but that is not what this show is about.)

It occurred to me that perhaps white women feminists, no less than white women generally, cannot imagine black women have vaginas. Or if they can, where imagination leads them is too far to go.

However, to think of black women as women is impossible if you cannot imagine them with vaginas. Sojourner Truth certainly had a vagina, as note her lament about her children, born of her body, but sold into slavery. Note her comment (straightforward, not bathetic) that when she cried out with a mother's grief, none but Jesus heard her. Surely a vagina has to be acknowledged when one reads these words. (A vagina the colour of raspberries and blackberries – or scuppernongs and muscadines – and of that strong, silvery sweetness, with, as well, a sharp flavour of salt.)

And through that vagina, Children.

Perhaps it is the black woman's children, whom the white woman – having more to offer her own children, and certainly not having to offer them slavery or a slave heritage or poverty or hatred, generally speaking: segregated schools, slum neighbourhoods, the worst of everything – resents. For they must always make her feel guilty. She fears knowing that black women want the best for their children just as she does. But she also knows black children are to have less in this world so that her children, white children, will have more (in some countries, all).

Better then to deny that the black woman has a vagina. Is capable of motherhood. Is a woman.

So, our mother thought, cradling her baby with one hand, while grading student papers with the other (she found teaching extremely compatible with childcare), the forces of the opposition are in focus. Fortunately, she had not once believed that all white women who called themselves feminists were any the less racist, because work after ambitious work issued from the country's presses and, with but a few shining examples (and our mother considered Tillie Olsen's *Silences* the *most* shining), white women feminists revealed themselves as incapable as white and black men of comprehending blackness and feminism in the same body, not to mention within the same imagination. By the time Ellen Moers's book *Literary Women: The Great Writers* was published in 1976 – with Lorraine Hansberry used as a token of what was not to be included, even in the future, in women's literature – our mother was well again. Exchanges like the following, which occurred wherever she was invited to lecture, she handled with aplomb:

*

WHITE STUDENT FEMINIST: Do you think black women artists should work in the black community?'

OUR MOTHER: 'At least for a period in their lives. Perhaps a couple of years, just to give back some of what has been received.'

WHITE STUDENT FEMINIST: 'But if you say that black women should work in the black community, you are saying that race comes before sex. What about black *feminists*? Should *they* be expected to work in the black community? And if so, isn't this a betrayal of their feminism? Shouldn't they work with women?'

OUR MOTHER: 'But of course black people come in both sexes.'

(Pause, while largely white audience, with sprinkle of perplexed blacks, ponders this possibility.)

In the preface to Ellen Moers's book, she writes: 'Just as we are now trying to make sense of women's literature in the great feminist decade of the 1790s, when Mary Wollstoncraft blazed and died, and when, also, Mme de Stael came to England and Jane Austen came of age, so the historians of the future will try to order women's literature of the 1960s and 1970s. They will have to consider Sylvia Plath as a woman writer and as a poet; but what will they make of her contemporary compatriot, the playwright Lorraine Hansberry? Born two years before Plath, and dead two years after her in her early thirties, Hansberry was not a suicide but a victim of cancer; she eloquently affirmed life, as Plath brilliantly wooed death. *Historians of the future will undoubtedly be satisfied with the title of Lorraine Hansberry's posthumous volume* (named not by Hansberry, but by her former husband who became executor of her estate), *To Be Young, Gifted and Black*;

and they will talk of her admiration for Thomas Wolfe; but of Sylvia Plath they will have to say 'young, gifted *and a woman*' (my italics).

It is, apparently, inconvenient, if not downright mind straining, for white women scholars to think of black women *as women*, perhaps because 'woman' (like 'man' among white males) is a name *they* are claiming for themselves, and themselves alone. Racism decrees that if *they* are now women (years ago they were ladies, but fashions change) then black women must, perforce, be something else. (While they were 'ladies', black women could be 'women', and so on.)

In any case, Moers expects 'historians of the future' to be as dense as those in the past, and at least as white. It doesn't *occur* to her that they might be white women with a revolutionary rather than a reactionary or liberal approach to literature, let alone *black* women. Yet many are bound to be. Those future historians, working-class black and white women, should have no difficulty comprehending: 'Lorraine Hansberry – Young, Gifted, Black, Activist, Woman, Eloquent Affirmer of Life'; and 'Sylvia Plath – Young, Gifted, White, Nonactivist Woman (in fact, fatally self-centred), Brilliant Wooer of Death.'

Of Our Mother's Continued Pilgrimage Towards Truth at the Expense of Vain Pride, or: One More River to Cross

It was a river she did not even know was there. Hence her difficulty in crossing it.

Our mother was glad, during the period of the above revelations – all eventually salutary to her mental health – to have occasion to address a large group of educated and successful black women. She had adequate respect for both education and success, since both were often needed, she thought, to comprehend the pains and anxieties of women who have neither. She spoke praisingly of black herstory; she spoke as she often did, deliberately, of her mother (formerly missing from both literature and history); she spoke of the alarming rise in the suicide rate of young black women all over America. She asked that these black women address themselves to this crisis. Address themselves, in effect, to themselves.

Our mother was halted in mid-speech. She was told she made too much of black herstory. That she should not assume her mother represented poor mothers all over the world (which she did assume) and she was told that those to address were black men; that, though it appeared more black women than men were committing suicide, still everyone knew black women to be the stronger of these two. Those women who committed suicide were merely sick, apparently with an imaginary or in any case a causeless disease. Furthermore, our mother was told: 'Our men must be supported in every way, *whatever they do*.' Since so many of 'our men' were doing little at the time but denigrating black women (and especially such educated and 'successful' black women as those assembled), when they deigned to recognise them at all, and since this denigration and abandonment were direct causes of at least some of the suicides, our mother was alarmed.

However, our mother did not for one moment consider becoming something other than black and female She was in the condition of twin 'afflictions' for life. And, to tell the truth, she rather enjoyed being more difficult things in one lifetime than anybody else. She was, in her own obstacle-crazed way, a snob.

But it was while recuperating from this blow to her complete trust in *all* black women (which was foolish, as all categorical trust is, of course) that she began to understand a simple principle: people do not wish to appear foolish; to avoid the appearance of foolishness, they were willing actually to remain fools. This led directly to a clearer grasp of many black women's attitudes about the women's movement.

They had seen, perhaps earlier than she (she was notorious for her optimism regarding any progressive group effort), that white 'feminists' are very often indistinguishable in their behaviour from any other white persons in America. She did not blame white *feminists* for the overturned buses of schoolchildren from Baton Rouge to Boston, as many black women did, or for the black schoolchildren beaten and spat upon. But look, just look, at the recent exhibit of women painters at the Brooklyn Museum!

('Are there no black women painters represented here?' one asked a white woman feminist.

'It's a *women's* exhibit!' she replied.)

Of the need for internationalism, alignment with non-Americans, non-Europeans, and non-chauvinists and against male supremacists or white supremacists wherever they exist on the globe, with an appreciation of all white American feminists who know more of non-white women's herstory than 'And Ain't I a Woman?' by Sojourner Truth

There was never a time when someone spoke of 'the women's movement' that our mother thought this referred only to the women's movement in America. When she thought of women moving, she automatically thought of women all over the world. She recognised that to contemplate the women's movement in isolation from the rest of the world would be – given the racism, sexism, elitism, and ignorance of so many American feminists – extremely defeating of solidarity among women, as well as depressing to the most optimistic spirit. Our mother had travelled and had every reason to understand that women's freedom was an idea whose time had come, and that it was an idea sweeping the world.

The women of China 'hold up half the sky'. They, who once had feet the size of pickles. The women of Cuba, fighting the combined oppression of African and Spanish macho, know that their revolution will be 'shit' if they are the ones to do the laundry, dishes, and floors after working all day, side by side in factory and field with their men, 'making the revolution'. The women of Angola, Mozambique, and Eritrea have picked up the gun and, propped against it, demand their right to fight the enemy within as well as the enemy without. The enemy within is the patriarchal system that has kept women virtual slaves throughout memory.

Our mother understood that in America white women who are truly feminist – for whom racism is inherently an impossibility – are largely outnumbered by *average* American white women for whom racism, inasmuch as it assures white privilege, is an accepted way of life. Naturally, many of these women, to be trendy, will leap to the feminist banner because it is now the place to be seen. What was required of women of colour was to learn to distinguish between who was the real feminist and who was not, and to exert energy in feminist collaborations only when there is little risk of wasting it. The rigours of this discernment will inevitably keep throwing women of colour back upon themselves, where there is, indeed, so much work, of a feminist nature, to be done. From the stopping of clitoridectomy and 'female circumcision' in large parts of Arabia and Africa to the heating of freezing urban tenements in which poor mothers and children are trapped alone to freeze to death. From the encouragement of women artists in Latin America to the founding of feminist publications for women of colour in North America. From the stopping of pornography, child slavery, forced prostitution, and molestation of minors in the home and in Times Square to the defence of women beaten and raped each Saturday night the world over, by their husbands.

To the extent that black women dissociate themselves from the women's movement, they abandon their responsibilities to women throughout the world. This is a serious abdication from and misuse of radical black herstorical tradition: Harriet Tubman, Sojourner Truth, Ida B. Wells, and Fannie Lou Hamer would not have liked it. Nor do I.

*From my journal, Jackson, Mississippi, June 15, 1972:
If one lives long enough, nothing will seem very important, or the past very painful. (This will seem truer on some days than on others.)*

Rebecca said today: 'I can cook soup, and eggs, and windows!'

She also said, while drawing letters on the kitchen table: 'A, O, and C.' Then, 'Oh-oh, the O is upside down!'

I feel very little guilt about the amount of time 'taken from my daughter' by my work. I was amazed that she could exist and I could read a book at the same time. And that she easily learned that there are other things to enjoy besides myself. Between an abstracted, harassed adult and an affectionate sitter or neighbour's child who can be encouraged to return a ball, there is no contest.

There *was* a day when, finally, after five years of writing *Meridian* (a book 'about' the Civil Rights Movement, feminism, socialism, the shakiness of revolutionaries, and the radicalisation of saints – the kind of book out of the political 1960s that white feminist scholar Francine du Plessix Gray declared recently in the *New York Times Book Review* did not exist), I felt a pang.

I wrote this self-pitying poem:

> Now that the book is finished,
> now that I know my characters will live,
> I can love my child again.
> She need sit no longer
> at the back of my mind
> the lonely sucking of her thumb
> a giant stopper in my throat.

But this was as much celebration as anything. After all, the book *was* finished, the characters *would* live, and of course I'd loved my daughter all along. As for 'a giant stopper in my throat', perhaps it is the fear of falling silent, *mute*, that writers have from time to time. This fear is a hazard of the work itself, which requires a *severity* towards the self that is often overwhelming in its discomfort, more than it is the existence of one's child, who, anyway, by the age of seven, at the latest, is one's friend, and can be told of the fears one has, that she can, by listening to one, showing one a new dance step, perhaps, sharing a colouring book, or giving one a hug, help allay.

In any case, it is not my child who tells me: I have no femaleness white women must affirm. Not my child who says: I have no rights black men must respect.

It is not my child who has purged my face from history and herstory and left mystory just that, a mystery; my child loves my face and would have it on every. page, if she could, as I have loved my own parents' faces above all others, and have refused to let them be denied, or myself to let them go.

Not my child, who in a way *beyond* all this, but really of a piece with it, destroys the planet daily, and has begun on the universe.

We are together, my child and I. Mother and child, yes, but *sisters* really, against whatever denies us all that we are.

For a long time I had this sign, which I constructed myself, deliberately, out of false glitter, over my desk:

> Dear Alice,
> Virginia Woolf had madness;
> George Eliot had ostracism,
> somebody else's husband,
> and did not dare to use
> her own name.
> Jane Austen had no privacy
> and no love life.
> The Brontë sisters never went anywhere
> and died young
> and dependent on their father.

Zora Hurston (ah!) had no money
and poor health.

You have Rebecca – who is
much more delightful
and less distracting
than any of the calamities
above.

1 Except for this plate and the choice of Sacajawca (who led
   Lewis and Clark on their Western expedition) as the subject of
   the Native American plate, I loved Chicago's art and audacity.

Susan Wilson
Living a Life

My story starts with my antipodean background. My mother and father both lost their parents when young. The Great Depression marked them. I was born just a few years after the return of the SS *Mooltan*, which brought my father and all the hundreds of returned servicemen back to the Wellington docks and the sound of the Maori waiata being sung on the wharves.

My father and other members of my family, although from a Scottish background, were Maori speakers and my father took me to Ohope Marae (the tribal meeting ground) when I was a teenager. Some of my cousins are Maori and my ideas about the family are deeply influenced by Maori culture and ideas.

I was a young woman in days of heady prosperity. Some British readers would not have been as well off as we were in the South Pacific in the 1970s. In the laid-back seaside climate of a small country I went surfing after school, embraced alternative culture, and helped lead and initiate many left-wing initiatives. At first these involvements seemed to free me but in the end they constrained and limited any growth of my ideas. The Left became Maoist, and Stalinist intolerance of any ideas that ran counter to the party line made life difficult. I was present at the founding of Nga Tamatoa, the Maori campaigning group in the 1970s and I thought seriously of marrying my then boyfriend, Tame Iti, and living in Ruatoki and learning Maori. I know now I was trying to escape Auckland's alternative culture and I needed to be somewhere else, be it Ruatoki or Lima, Peru, a place that had always had a fascination for me. In the end I decided on South America. Late one March night I caught a flight to Tahiti – leaving Auckland in a state of grief, confused and unable to understand why I was leaving a land I loved so well. I cried in the limpid clear blue Gauguin lagoons for three days then boarded a plane for Lima and the absolute unknown. It was a traumatic separation. I had never been outside New Zealand before. But the shock of Lima and its baroque architecture was exhilarating: the city was beautiful, and the churches and palaces, the sound of spoken Spanish led me in an entirely different direction, one I continue to follow. These things made me a painter, made it possible. I was wrenched permanently from my previous world and given an experience of another, much bigger, older, post-colonial world. This set me imagining and dreaming.

My attitude to having children was coloured by my parents' experiences. My paternal grandmother died of septicaemia days after giving birth at home in rural New Zealand. My father told her story:

I have clear recollections of Christmas 1923. I was five and a half: For the Christmas party Dad dressed up as Father Christmas and Mother seemed so anxious to have a delightful day. She died on 30 Dec that year. Maybe I knew a baby was expected – if so subsequent events completely overshadowed that. Lewis and I were in the cherry plum tree eating plums. Somebody, perhaps Dad, called us inside. We went into our front bedroom to say goodbye to Mother. Perhaps I was told she was dying of blood poisoning. Death was not a word I understood. Did I kneel beside the bed? Did Mother want to bless us in turn – she waited to give us some special farewell as after Lewis, I knelt beside the bed. We were taken to the kitchen. My father had a big left hand into which he sobbed and Kate Rudd told me to go and play and dinner would be ready soon.

Maybe it was New Year's Eve 1923 that the undertaker came. At the front door, at Dad's wish, I saw a little girl, Jean Nisbet Wilson in my mother's arms in a coffin. The baby seemed bonny and death did not deny me the persistent reality of that scene. For some years I had vague ideas I'd see mother again – her love and kindly cheerful humour would return.

I was also very affected by reading Simone de Beauvoir and by her choice to remain childless. The idea of her relationship with Sartre, the intellectual companionship, was all beguiling. That was the kind of life I wished for, not a domestic, suburban or rural one. And I was afraid of childbirth. Frankly I was afraid it would kill me. I've never been naïve about the risks of giving birth; my mother was a maternity nurse who worked as a midwife during the war years, so I always knew there could be complications. One of my closest friends gave birth to a baby with spina bifida when I was living in London in the 1970s. I remember the nappies putrifying in the washing machine while she lay in bed doing nothing for days on end, sunk in the deepest of depressions. Her solution to her misery and our youthful inability to comprehend it was to become a junkie. We were all confused. We'd been subjected to the anti-family propaganda of pop and alternative culture and felt we were supposed to despise the traditional family set-up, and our parents.

In 1976 I began a long-standing friendship with a disillusioned Israeli who had been brought up on a radical kibbutz in a 'group of age'. At three days old she had been taken from her mother to a communal nursery and lived there throughout her childhood. Her mother visited her each afternoon for a strictly limited period. It seemed the answer to all my dreams. But when I got to know her well, I saw that she was shot through with a deep sense of lost intimacy and lost mothering. She craved being near her parents.

I also remember walking around Holland Park with a friend as she told me that she had terminated five pregnancies. Choice became problematic; you were able to control your fertility and choose 'when' or 'never' or you could endlessly delay. I was very keen to devote myself to painting and to ideas. I wanted to go and live in Spain. I fancied going with my new husband to Barcelona to live alongside a group of poets and writers who seemed to be having a wonderful life in the Barrio Gotico. I felt stuck in London.

These were unhappy and difficult years; crazy ideas of 'biological chauvinism' abounded, that it did not matter who had fathered a child, that it was chauvinistic to ascribe paternity to the biological father. What unhappiness ensued! There was nothing new or bold or utopian about this world.

I retreated to the world of paint, and fell in love with painting from the past, with the poetry of Mantegna, of Giovanni Bellini and Piero Della

Francesca. My husband and I cycled across Italy looking at altarpieces. I remember cycling across to find the *Madonna dell Parto* at Monterchi. After leaning my bike against the wall of the little church I went inside and was confronted by the serene loveliness of Piero's pregnant Virgin. There were many trips to see paintings I had come to know from books, from art school lectures and from other artists' conversations. I kept on working in my studio, I had shows, I travelled and I taught.

Then in 1986, on holiday in Barcelona, I realised I was pregnant with our child. I remember going up to the top of Montserrat in the cable car and eating an oily dish of chicken and chips. Looking out over Catalonia I wondered just what would happen to me now. The day was clear and you could see for miles over the canyons, buttes and mesas, rippling mile upon purply mile towards the Pyrenees.

When the children were born I didn't want to say 'this is my space, and my time' and exclude them. From the start I encouraged them to draw on the walls and floor in the studio. It was one place where you were free as a bird to make a mess. I gave them good paper if they wanted it – and I also began to pay them to sit for me for quick portraits if they wanted something from the shops.

When I was a child my father had had a study where he wrote his sermons and prepared for his work, and I liked very much to go in and occupy the floor, have a little play or look at the ashtray he had made from lava taken from the slopes of Vesuvius when he vOs a stretcher-bearer in 1944. I was made welcome and usually didn't stay very long. The room

I remember as a private, intellectual space, full of books and papers, curiosities on the shelves, a rosy patterned carpet on the floor. It was different to every other room. It was full of ideas. It was also another world far from the gardens, the farms and the sheep.

When the children were small we paid for childcare while I went away to work. For the first few months of my daughter's life my husband had a small amount of paternity leave and so took care of her, sterilising bottles and changing nappies one day a week while I went up to Wolverhampton to teach on the BA painting course there. He was very good but he had to cope with the bottles and sterilisation which I never had to contend with as I was breast-feeding. At work I expressed milk at lunchtime in the first aid room and brought it back down with me for my next scheduled absence. I never told anybody I had a baby until the end of year show. My punchy, tough boss, Knighton Hoskings, was overjoyed at my daughter's arrival and said I had been silly not to tell him. Later we did a tutorial with my son present. He was extremely active and we had a lot of difficulty restraining him from tearing around the room: Knighton rightly noted that the students saw us as frailer and more human.

I did a series of cot paintings of my son asleep for a show at Cadogan Contemporary which the *Spectator* reviewed in 1992. This subject had overwhelmed me, eclipsing all other subject matters; I was as besotted by the boy as I had been by his sister before him and he slept so soundly every night it was relatively easy to make the pictures. These paintings were presented to the Patrons of New Art at the Tate Gallery, the *Guardian* wrote a review and later I was interviewed by Louisa Buck on the Radio 3 programme *Night Waves*, where I described how and why these pictures were made. As a result of all this the Usher Gallery in Lincoln asked me to work on 'Reclaiming the Madonna', a survey show about artists as mothers. Janita Elton, the exhibitions officer, and I travelled all over the UK visiting artists to select work. This was a great journey. We learned a lot about the practice of painting, and were impressed by the determination of the artists we met. There were seminars and debates at the ICA and the exhibition was chosen to launch the new Museum of Women's Art project.

The genesis of the show lay in my dissatisfaction with the Ikon Gallery's exhibition in 1990, called 'Mothers'. I liked the idea of it enormously, but it did not examine the way motherhood affects the creative woman. And the thorny nettle – that of making affectionate and loving art about children and babies – was not grasped at all. It still seems to me that there must be a place for the portrayal of the idyllic, for there is a part of motherhood which for some of us is the most overwhelming love affair. Childbirth and the rearing of children are core material: for many women: they cannot be put aside, but inform and affect all creativity.

The show was popular and it did a long and successful tour which demonstrated the high level of interest and support for this particular subject. The Usher Gallery made purchases of work and provided tremendous commitment and enthusiasm but we had, somehow, hoped for more. For more things to change perhaps.

Being an artist and a mother isn't an easy existence.

Over the years I've tried to be adventurous and take risks. I did several solo shows abroad and took both the work and the children. My daughter and son were very small and it was a mighty struggle. I would lie in bed at night feeling as though I would burst simply with the logistics of it all. I used one of those folding cots so that in Pisa or Auckland my son would go to bed each night seeing the same pattern around him. At this time both my husband and I were freelancers with a mortgage to pay. Neither of us could stop working as both of our incomes were needed. On several occasions I made large sums of money which saved the family from mortgage arrears and debt. I have always tried to weave together family, work and making money. I have no idea what my children will think of it when they are grown up.

Another artist, Stanley Palmer, brought up two very small children on his own after his wife died. 'The thing is they have to get used to there just being one of you. It gets easier,' he said gamely as I boarded a twenty-four-hour flight back to England with a baby and a three-year-old. The shows were a success and I sold well, got reviews and made contacts.

In 1993 I took up an award with the British School at Rome. I was very determined to go but as it is very much a place for contemplation, academic research and debate, it isn't possible to take small children there. At the time my children were only two and five, so we stayed in a remote house on a mountainside in the Abruzzi instead. There were snakes in the garden and scorpions in the house. A rat lived in the cooker and crickets flew about the rooms. At night fireflies danced among the trees. The children loved the place with a passion. Each evening we would sit looking out over the Mainarde mountains watching the sun go down. My father and my uncle had been in this area during the war. I was never going to be the same person after I saw the battlefield at Monte Cassino which lies just over the range, and came to grips with what my father and the other men had endured. Going to Cassino awakened my interest in heroism, masculinity, bravery. Germaine Greer writing in the *Guardian* on 16 May 1994, at the time of the D-Day commemorations, said: 'I came very gradually to the realisation that there is a great debt unpaid and that there is barely time to pay it.'

In 1996 I worked on a survey show of women's self-portraits: 'In the Looking Glass', with Janita Elton from the Usher Gallery and Dr Judith Collins, twentieth-century curator of British art at the Tate Gallery. We went and talked to a cross-section of contemporary artists working around the country ranging from new graduates such as Isobel Brigham, to more established artists such as Jean Cooke and Maggi Hambling. The show did a long tour and had good reviews. Germaine Greer gave an excellent, scholarly lecture and opened the exhibition, which still carries resonance for me. The idea for this show came from 'Reclaiming the Madonna': as we looked at the work women showed us we came upon many good self-portraits – too many just to ignore.

Despite all this I am now less optimistic than I was back in the days when I curated 'Reclaiming the Madonna'. For example, I think I was, at that time, hopeful that a generation of well-paid, high-flying city women would support women in the arts. But I guess they are too bent on quality time with their children when they get home exhausted. Like many women in my position, I was not able to consolidate a position in the several art schools where I worked as a visiting lecturer. Like many part-time art lecturers in British universities, I was a woman with children and had to go home to relieve the childminder. In this sort of post you don't get paid sabbaticals or research time; I could never go after work to the pub. But like Mario Vargas Llosa, who writes so vehemently about bohemianism and the ruin of creative Peruvians through drinking, I also had a horror of the hours spent at the bar being clever and pissed. Vargas Llosa saw that the only way to be a writer was indeed to write.

One of my female colleagues – in my last days at a London college – pointed out that nobody on the painting staff had children except her and me. 'You know what it means,' she said. 'One, they have absolutely no commitment to the future, and two, you and I will get the chop.' We did.

Too soon my children will be children no longer. As they have grown the issue of support with homework, with projects and interests has grown. The older they are, the more you must do. When my mother died I reflected that nobody ever again would be as interested or care as much about what I did as my mother. Nobody would bother to get as cross with me, or take so much pleasure in my arrival. If a mother doesn't provide the support, it is unlikely that anyone else will.

My most recent project has been illustrating, with a series of large paintings, Katharine Mansfield's short stories for the Folio Society. It has been a great experience. A short deadline, just nine months, in which to make eleven paintings which adhere closely to the text. I have never painted from memory or imagination so it has been challenging to change my way of working. First, I went on a long summer holiday with my family to Port de la Selva, near Cape Creus in Catalonia. For two weeks we lived a rough existence in a tent: cooking over one little burner and walking everywhere we went. It was great to walk to town along the clifftops above the sea, and stop if the water looked exciting, have a swim for a few hours, then head on for drinks and ice creams; to climb the high steep hills covered in thyme oak, blackberry and sage brush, dodging through the scrubby foliage and up over the seemingly abandoned terraced walls.

Down on the beach I would sit and draw for hours at a time, watching the holiday-makers. The way the bathers flung down their towels and rushed into the water, dived, languished, floated and quietly celebrated that sparkling, clear Catalan water reminded me of my childhood world – the New Zealand beach, so well described by Mansfield in 'At the Bay'. By the time we left, the children were very good at snorkelling, had seen little squid shooting around in someone else's bucket, had caught their own shellfish and starfish, and fought and squabbled. They had ridden very fast in a big inflatable boat around the Cape Creus, to those wild rocky shores where the rock is indeed piled up like shit in the lumps, swirls and encrustations that Buñuel and Dalí filmed in *L'Age d'Or*. Tiny chinks in rocks reveal deep clear green harbours where you can see the shells on the bottom thirty feet below. Small shacks *a refugio* stand beneath a single bowed pine – a place for fisherman to weather out a storm.

Back in London I got out my books of drawings and set to work to conjure up this world of sparkling sea. There had been one day when the water had been shiny silver and a strong onshore wind had sent big bashing waves, which made some little children afraid, crashing on to the beach. Plump old women revelled in the flying wind and turbulent sea and fought each wave. I sat on the beach and fought the paper, making drawing upon drawing of each figure: the skinny kids, the plump matrons, the languid mothers glad of nothing to do. The men sitting, knees bent or leaning back on one elbow, all carefree and saturated with warmth. The holiday that seems as though it will never end.

The thing is, I don't think I could have made these paintings if I hadn't had the children. I'd have been too impatient. I'd have wanted to be in the city, on the Ramblas in Barcelona drinking coffee – in the Bar Zurich maybe – and looking at art, drawing art, thinking about art, not unlike the literary gentleman finely depicted by Mansfield in 'Life of Ma Parker'. In this story the cleaning lady comes to do for a man who is clearly part of the Bloomsbury set:

'A baker, Mrs Parker!' the literary gentleman would say. For occasionally he laid aside his tomes and lent an ear, at least, to this product called Life. 'It must be rather nice to be married to a baker!'

Mrs Parker didn't look so sure.

'Such a clean trade,' said the gentleman.

Mrs Parker didn't look convinced.[1]

Life. I had to be forced into changing my existence, and having children does that to you. You are never the same again. I was forced by their needs to go on a beach holiday, something their father and I hadn't done in years. I don't sunbathe and I don't have a bikini. But you see it was lovely just to sit and listen to the sea, to be by the beach night and day with my family. And they took a keen interest in my project and watched the ideas developing.

After all, they have grown up with me in my studio and have always given me good advice. When they sensed I was lagging behind they pushed me forward. My son checked on my progress, wanting to know what I had done and how it was going. He would tell me what he liked and what he didn't like.

I had become involved in life; I was not a mere spectator. And I was able to make two very good pictures of the sea. This might signal a beginning, a new departure for me. I think I now know how to paint the landscape of my childhood.

Luisa Dilner, the doctor who has a column in the *Guardian*, says you can't really have it all. She observed that a new breed of women were determined to do it all, not to hand their child to the nanny even when they had plenty of money. Dilner pointed out, however, that you have to create time and space if you want to work . It seems there's a swing back to hands-on mothering – even Madonna says she likes to do the chores. So where does that leave grumbling me? I'm not so keen on chores: I'm not wild about having to search for a sock, or being told that I should've sewn up a pair of tracksuit bottoms. Or realising at the school gate that the lunchbox languishes miles away on the bench and that I'm going to have to go back for it. But there are visual treats, visual ideas, that catch your eye continually and get woven into a painting. As my children and I rounded a corner this week, along swung several rows of rebellious girls from my daughter's school, all in trousers so big you could fit at least three people in each pair, the frayed cuffs dragging in the dust. Long blond plaits trailed innocently past the odd spiked collar. 'Those,' said my daughter severely, 'are the goths. We are all afraid of them.'

This is where I find my ideas. I find them on my way around my area, living a life. I can't possibly separate life out and shut it off. I want to paint the faces I see on the local bus. I look hard and well wherever I go, and watch people wherever I am. I take a sketch book around with me and make little drawings and notes. Increasingly I exhibit these in exhibitions. At the time of writing I have a request for six such pictures to go on show at Drumcroon Art Gallery in Lancashire.

Would I have been an artist without children? Yes, but a different one. A previous headmistress at my daughter's school, when asked about work and children, uttered a glorious concept: 'Use the interstices of time.' That's what I was doing on the beach, using the interstices of time, making art from life.

1 From 'Life of Ma Parker' in *The Garden Party and Other Stories*, Katherine Mansfield, Constable & Co., 1992.

Permissions

'Imagining Motherhood' by Julia Alvarez, published in *Something to Declare*, Algonquin Books of Chapel Hill, 1998. Copyright © 1982, 1998 by Julia Alvarez. Reprinted by permission of Susan Bergholz Literary Services, New York. All rights reserved.

A shorter version of 'Small Beauties' by Julia Darling appeared in *MsLexia*, no. 1, Spring 1999, entitled 'Good Writers Make Bad Mothers'.

Excerpt from *The Blue Jay's Dance* by Louise Erdrich. Copyright © 1995 by Louise Erdrich. Reprinted by arrangement with HarperCollins Publishers, Inc.

Claudette Johnson's essay, 'How Many do you Have Now?' appeared in the catalogue *Reclaiming the Madonna: Artists as Mothers* accompanying the exhibition of the same name organised by the Usher Gallery, Lincoln, in 1993.

Excerpt from *The Diary and Letters of Käthe Kollwitz*, translated by Krishna Winston. Copyright © 1988 by Northwestern University Press. Used by permission of Krishna Winston.

Excerpt from 'Anger and Tenderness' from *Of Woman Born: Motherhood as Experience and Institution* by

Biographical Notes

Julia Alvarez
Julia Alvarez was born in the Dominican Republic and moved to the United States with her family when she was ten. Her poetry includes *Homecoming* and *The Other Side: El Otro Lado*. Her novel *How the Garcia Girls Lost Their Accents* won the PEN Oakland/Josephine Miles Award in 1990. Her works include another novel, *In the Time of Butterflies* and a collection of short stories *AYo!*

Ellen Bell
Ellen Bell is a professional artist and lives with her husband in Cambridge.

PJ Crook
PJ Crook is a figurative painter who lives and works in Gloucestershire. She exhibits in this country, the USA, France and Canada with her dealers Theo Waddington and Alain Blondel. In 1996, Cheltenham Art Gallery organised a retrospective exhibition that toured museums in the UK and France and, in 2001, the Morohashi Museum of Modern Art in Japan presented a survey of her paintings from their important collection of her work. Other public collections include the Imperial War Museum; City of Paris, Ralli Institute, Geneva; Department of

Transport, London; El Mundo, Madrid; Havatz, Tel Aviv; Royal West of England Academy; and J P Morgan Inc. Private collections are held by Paul Allen, Jackie Collins, Robert Fripp, Toyah Willcox, Victor Chandler, Christie Brinkley, Philip Kotler, Hollie Johnson, Peter Gabriel, Nicholas de Rothschild and Sir Anthony Bamford.

Julia Darling

Julia Darling is a playwright, and a writer of short and long fiction. Her short stories have appeared in many anthologies and she is currently compiling a second collection of stories following the publication of her first, *Bloodlines*. Her first novel *Crocodile Soup* was published in 1998 by Transworld and has subsequently been published in Canada and America, and translated in Danish. She is working on her second novel and a new play, and is currently Writer in Residence at Newcastle University. She lives in Newcastle with her two daughters.

Silvia Ebert

The second of three children, Silvia Ebert was born in 1926 while her family were living in Rome, but was educated at a Quaker School in Buckinghamshire and then at Cheltenham Ladies' College. Her first engagement as a dancer was in Nöel Coward's revue *Sigh No More*, followed by appearances with The Royal Ballet, the Ballet Theatre of New York at Covent Garden, 'Bullet in the Ballet' (choreographed by Massine), the Glyndebourne Festival Opera, Intimate Revues, pantomimes including 'Cinderella' with Julie Andrews, a floor show with Audrey Hepburn, 'Carousel', and various films and TV performances. In 1951 she married Peter Ebert, opera director and administrator, and as a result lived in Germany for two periods of eight years while Peter worked as Intendant for various theatres. She has eight children – five boys and three girls – plus two stepdaughters, and now lives in a restored farmhouse in Umbria, Italy.

Louise Erdrich

Louise Erdrich is of German-American and Chippewa descent. Her novels include *Love Medicine*, *The Beet Queen*, *Tracks*, *The Bingo Palace* and *Tales of Burning Love*. She co-authored another novel, *The Crown of Columbus*, with her husband, Michael Dorris, and has published two collections of poetry – *Jacklight* and *Baptism of Desire*.

Maggie Gee

Maggie Gee has written eight novels including *Dying in Other Words*, *The Burning Book*, *Grace*, *Where are the Snows*, and most recently *The Ice People*. She also writes about fiction, science and the visual arts for the *Telegraph* and *The Sunday Times* among others. She has been married for eighteen years to the writer and broadcaster Nicholas Rankin, Rosa's father.

Laura Godfrey-Isaacs

Laura Godfrey-Isaacs is an artist, Research Fellow in Fine Art at The Kent Institute of Art and Design, and Director of 'home'. home is a new arts organisation based inside a family house in Camberwell, London. Renovated over two years, the house has not been touched since the 1930s and is built on a curious pentagon design. Instead of clearing the rooms so they operate as a gallery, the living environment of the house is used, providing fifteen unique spaces in which to hold a variety of exhibitions and events, and to generate publications and related offsite projects.

Claudette Johnson

Claudette Johnson has a small 'space' studio in East London. Her most recent shows include an exhibition at Deborah House in 1999, a group show, 'Transforming the Crown', in New York in 1998, and a solo show, 'Portraits from a Small Room', in 1995. In 1999 she was selected to produce a portrait of Maya Angelou for her 70th birthday (sadly the final work was never made due to time restraints). She no longer teaches.

Nicole Ward Jouve

Nicole Ward Jouve was born and bred in Provence, France, but has lived all her adult life in Britain. She tends to write fiction, autobiography and family history in French, and essays in English – but this neat bi-lingual pattern is changing! She has written books on: Baudelaire, Colette, a study of the Yorkshire Ripper Case (*The Streetcleaner*, Marion Boyars, 1987), thoughts on her own writing and gender (*The Semi-transparent Envelope*, co-authored with Sue Roe and Susan Sellers, Marion Boyars, 1994), stories in various collections including her own – *Shades of Grey*, Virago, 1981, and one novel in French – *L'Entremise*. Her most recent book is *Female Genesis: Creativity, Self and Gender* (Polity Press, 1998). She is Professor of Literature and Women's Studies at York University and is currently working on a family history.

Beeban Kidron

Before becoming a filmmaker, Beeban was a waitress, dancing girl, courier and shop worker. She has been taking photographs since the age of 11 and was 'discovered' aged 13 by Magnum photographer Evie Arnold. Her work on films such as *Oranges are Not the Only Fruit*, *To Wong Foo*, *Thanks For Everything*, *Great Moments in Aviation*, and *Used People* has attracted many awards including The Prix Italia, several British Academy awards, a Golden Hugo, critics choice at Creitel and Lillian Gish award. Her films have also been honoured at many film festivals including, Tokyo, London, Berlin, Toronto, Chicago, Telluride, San Francisco, Sydney and Venice. She lives in London and has two children.

Käthe Kollwitz

Käthe Kollwitz née Schmidt (1867–1945) was a German artist, born in East Prussia and educated in Munich and Berlin. Primarily a graphic artist, she also produced bronze and granite sculptures. Her husband, a doctor, ran a clinic in an impoverished area of Berlin and her work reflected her knowledge of the effects of social injustice. She produced series of prints including *Der Weberaufstand* (*Weavers' Revolt*) and *Bauernkrieg* (*Peasants' War*). Her youngest son, Peter, was killed in action during the First World War and after this her work often portrayed mothers attempting to protect their children. Her work was denounced by the Nazis and removed from exhibition. She died shortly before the end of the Second World War, having lost a beloved grandson in the fighting and much of her work when her studio was bombed.

Mary Lowe

Mary Lowe was born in Bath in 1959. She studied History at the University of York and has lived in Newcastle for the last fifteen years. Mary has done a variety of jobs including teaching, psychiatric nursing, health promotion and training. She writes plays, stories and poems and is soon to finish her MA in Creative Writing at the University of Northumbria.

Jacqueline Morreau

Jacqueline Morreau is a US-born figurative painter who has lived in London since 1972. Her works are in many public collections including the British Museum and the Arts Council of England. She has been active in promoting women's work through curating, writing and editing, beginning with the 1980 exhibition 'Women's Images of Men' at the ICA in London, and her collaboration in the book produced as a result of that exhibition. She is married with four children.

Kate Paul

Born in South India, Kate Paul was the youngest of five children, all girls. After studying English language and literature at Oxford, she worked as an actress for many years. Recently she has been writing audioguide scripts for galleries such as the National Portrait Gallery, the Wallace Collection and Tate Britain and at present is also deeply involved in sitting for her sister, the painter Celia Paul. Kate lives in South London.

Adrienne Rich

Adrienne Rich is an American essayist and poet. Her collections of poetry include: *Driving into the Wreck*, which won the National Book Award in 1974, *Dark Fields of the Republic: Poems 1991–1995* and *Midnight Salvage: Poems 1995–1998*. Her prose works include *What is Found There* and the influential *Of Woman Born: Motherhood as Experience and Institution* (1976; 1986).

Alice Walker

Alice Walker was born in Eatonton, Georgia and is the author of six novels, *The Color Purple*, *The Temple of My Familiar*, *Possessing the Secret of Joy*, *The Third Life of Grange Copeland*; *Meridian* and *By The Light of My Father's Smile*; two books of short stories, *In Love and Trouble* and *You Can't Keep a Good Woman Down*; four collections of essays and memoirs, *Anything we Love can be Saved*, *In Search of Our Mother's Gardens*, *Living by the Word* and *The Same River Twice*; and four volumes of poetry, *Horses Make a Landscape Look More Beautiful*, *Once*, *Revolutionary Petunias* and *Goodnight Willie Lee, I'll See You in the Morning*. She has received many awards including the Radcliffe Institute Medal and a Guggenheim fellowship. Her hugely popular novel *The Color Purple* won the American Book Award and the Pulitzer Prize and was made into a film by Steven Spielberg. Her most recent book is a powerful collection of stories *The Way Forward is with a Broken Heart* (The Women's Press, 2001).

Deborah Watson

Deborah Watson has had a varied career which has included working as a make-up artist and singing backing vocals for Barry Manilow. She now specialises in arts education, working as an arts development worker and running the children's charity The Honeyhive, which facilitates art workshops in schools and museums. Her work appeared in *The Women's Artists Diary* (1999).

Susan Wilson
Originally from the wilds of New Zealand's South Island, Susan Wilson was educated at Camberwell School of Art and the Royal Academy Schools. She co-curated 'Reclaiming the Madonna' and 'In the Looking Glass' touring exhibitions originating from the Usher Gallery in Lincoln. In 2000 she had her first solo show at Browse & Darby, Cork Street, London. She has just completed illustrating Katherine Mansfield's short stories for the Folio society. She lives in London.

Sue Woolfe
Sue Woolfe spent her childhood in the Blue Mountains of New South Wales. She was educated at Sydney University and the University of New England. She has made films, written textbooks and edited film subtitles, and has also written two novels – *Painted Woman* and *Leaning Towards Infinity* (The Women's Press, 1998). She has a daughter.